Now I See

A Mothers Memoir of Her Son's Miraculous Healing

Written By
Vanessa Clark

thrive
PUBLISHING

14 15 16 17 18   7 6 5 4 3 2 1

Now I See!
ISBN 978-0-9960032-4-7

Copyright ©2014 by Vanessa Clark
Thrive Edutainment, llc
1609 South Boston Ave. Suite 200 Tulsa, OK 74119

Cover photos:
Corey Lack, Corey Lack Pictures

Cover concept, typeset & design:
Christian Ophus, Emerge Publishing

Contents

Introduction

This book is not only about God's miraculous power intervening and changing my family and my life forever, but it is also about learning to hear and recognize that still small voice of God in our lives. Yes, this book is about the miraculous healing my son received from God, but the story doesn't start with his diagnosis or even with his birth.

In order to adequately tell the story of my son's healing, I must begin at the beginning of my life. God in His mysterious ways had, unknowingly to me, orchestrated many of the seemingly unimportant and mundane parts of my life to ultimately culminate in my son's healing. The events He put in motion long before my son was born would change my life and my family's life forever.

Chapter 1

In the Beginning

"For I know the plans I have for you, declares the Lord..."
(Jeremiah 29:11).

The tension in our home was heavy. It was present so often, you would think I would be accustomed to it by now, but that is like getting accustomed to war. It doesn't happen. Even if you get used to the daily reality of war, you always long for the day when peace will reign. Until then you learn to endure your environment the best you can and hold on to the hope that it can and will get better and the constant fighting will go away. That is the hope that I held onto.

I experienced glimpses of it in the constant ebb and flow in my parents' relationship. It seemed cyclical. Even as a young child, I could recognize the predictable, never-ending pattern of nagging, volatile explosions, brief or extended breakups, separations and threats of divorce followed by the inevitable dramatic reconciliation which to me only served to signal the beginning of a new cycle of the same pattern. But who knows, maybe this time it would be different.

"Why couldn't they just get along like other parents?" I pondered. Was it really that difficult? I didn't understand. I rationalized that deep down they must enjoy these battles; otherwise, they would just stop it. They were in fact the ones who controlled this explosive environment. Didn't they know that? I couldn't wait for the moment I could get away from all of them and escape into my bedroom, alone, undisturbed. There wasn't anything to look forward to, except escape. That was it. Just getting away.

The environment I was raised in was not a peaceful one, and yet I was loved by both of my parents. My home was simply filled with strife and unrest, seemingly endless fighting between the two adults who ruled it.

Dear Jesus, please help so that my parents will stop fighting . . . Dear Jesus, please help so that my parents will stop fighting . . . Dear Jesus, please help so that my parents will stop fighting. Surely at any moment it would stop, but it didn't. Usually not until it had escalated to a point of no return. This would result in one parent moving out as a separation or divorce was pursued. Then some weeks or months later my parents would make up and start a short-lived time of what I saw as a "honeymoon phase" before they repeated the same pattern again in a couple of months.

That was the way my parents lived their lives. I wondered, Why do I have to be a part of it? I looked over at my brother. Like me, he sat unnaturally quiet. We had mastered the art of not speaking, not moving, not doing anything that might upset that tiny amount of peace we longed to hold on to. But let me take you back to where I came into the picture . . .

I was born in San Diego, California, on April 26, 1981, the older of two children. From the outside, my family must have looked ideal. A beautiful mother who had appeared in various commercials and television programs as well as a handsome father who took pride in working hard at his job, taking meticulous care of our yard and flower beds and who enjoyed working out and taking care of his body. My brother Justin was just nineteen months younger than I, and although we had sibling spats from time to time, for the most part we were close to each other.

We looked to be the perfect family of four: my mom was striking with blonde hair, big brown eyes and an outgoing, vivacious personality that could take command of any situation. My father still played flag football from time to time with his friends. He had been a star football player in high school, and I remember my friends telling me he resembled Sylvester Stallone. I inherited the dark features of my dad, dark brown eyes and thick dark brown wavy hair. My brother was blond like my mother and had inherited my father's physical prowess, succeeding at every sport he played, joining traveling and all-star sports teams every year in almost every sport he played – soccer, baseball, basketball, roller hockey, etc.

Throughout my young life, I was enrolled in gymnastics, dance and had competed in local beauty pageants. Outwardly, we appeared financially capable as well. At one point my parents owned matching red and white BMW's, and at the age of seven I remember the excitement as our brand-new custom home was built, complete with a Jacuzzi which had a built-in waterfall overflowing into our in-ground pool. We also had a half basketball court in our backyard that my brother and Dad loved to compete on.

My parents were very involved in our lives. My mother always handpicked the schools we would attend as well as the teachers we would have. When I was young she would have the neighborhood kids over to play, dressing up and putting on talent shows in our backyard. She loved dolling me up in all the latest styles whether I was going to school or to a friend's birthday party... I was always dressed up.

I remember my dad was always a very dedicated worker, and he instilled in me the importance of a good work ethic. As long as I can remember, he worked nights or third shift and always provided for our family. At the same time, he always made time to practice and even help coach my brother's sports teams. In later years when I was in high school, both parents attended all my cheerleading competitions and worked tediously on weekends to help me raise the money needed to attend all my squad's events.

I was raised knowing that Jesus Christ had died on

the cross for my sins and was my Lord and Savior. I am told by my mother that I officially asked Jesus into my heart while watching a televised Billy Graham crusade with her at around the age of five. Billy Graham gave an invitation, and I informed my mom that I wanted to ask Jesus to come and live in my heart. I asked and He did.

While I was raised in a family that acknowledged Jesus as Lord, the constant fighting, strife and unrest that existed between my parents overshadowed every area of our home life and did not reflect this truth. Home was not a pleasant place to be. It was tense, stressful and at times violent.

I never remember us consistently attending a church, and I dreaded when we would randomly go because I didn't know anyone. It seems that the times we went were few and far between and always to a new place. I was a shy, self-conscious and unconfident child, and I was extremely uncomfortable being the new kid who didn't know anyone. I was easily embarrassed and unable to hide when I was as my entire face would quickly blush to a deep color red. I hated being singled out or attracting any attention to myself. In Sunday school, I just hoped to make it through class without being called on.

Adding to my anxiety was the fact that I never knew anything that we were expected to know in Sunday school. I specifically remember sitting on a wooden chair in a classroom across from a green chalkboard as kids were reciting and singing the books of the Bible. I was so fearful I would be called on. This might not have bothered anyone else, but having the personality of a "pleaser," I couldn't bear the thought of being singled out and unable to correctly answer the teacher, or to not even know what the class was talking about. I tried my best to avoid being called upon in Sunday school class.

Even though we were not church members, Jesus made an impact when He came to live in me. I do have memories of my brother and I being read Bible stories by my parents and being led in prayer before bed. Through the Lord equipping me with an innately trusting and believing spirit, the foundation was laid through these stories, prayers and my parents' explanation of God's will for me, to understand that Jesus loved and cared about me and could do anything I asked. I was not afraid to approach Jesus in prayer.

When I was in the sixth grade, I vividly remember having to locate an important school I.D. card as an extended school break came to an end. As far as I understood, this card was irreplaceable and I had already been looking fretfully for it throughout the school break. My room had been torn apart as I looked through drawers, under piles of papers and in jacket pockets. I prayed to God as I continued my search. Suddenly it occurred to me to look through an old purse that hung on the handle of my door. I rifled through it and there it was, within a pocket inside the purse! God helped me find my card! I was amazed. I still remember the sense of relief washing over me, and the realization hit me that God had answered my prayer. It was a miracle. It had been an insurmountable problem in my sixth grade life, but God had solved it.

The other memory of prayer I have is one that I prayed constantly. The exact words were, "Dear Jesus, please help so that my parents will stop fighting." It almost became sort of a game in my mind. I would repeat the prayer over and over and over as my parents fought. Then suddenly there would be a break in the action, and I would think, it worked! Then they would pick up again where they left off and my prayer would continue.

In sharing about my less than ideal home life, my intention is not to be hurtful to either of my parents who I know both love me; however, I think it is important to let you know how much the atmosphere I was raised in shaped me. To say that my parents could not get along would be an understatement. I cannot express the level of tension and hatred that existed and was communicated in our home. I would at times get physically sick due to the fighting and stress. My stomach would turn to knots.

To this day, my brother and I both are often described as "peace-keepers" and "pleasers." I believe that we adapted these skills due to our home environment. We just wanted the fighting to stop, so whatever we could do to aid in keeping the peace is what we leaned towards. This tendency grew to dominate much of my personality and has been demonstrated throughout my life. For me confrontation was unpleasant, and I always tried to do what I thought was right and would make the people around me happy.

It seemed as if my parents were always fighting, and

sometimes I wondered if they would ever stop. I would imagine my parents getting really old and thought surely by that time they would be living in peace with one another. I didn't recall seeing a lot of old people fight. Old people seemed to live quiet, peaceful lives. I rationalized that was because they were just too old to fight these all-consuming battles. But as I continued to grow up, the fighting did not stop. My parents fought brutally until they divorced later in life around the time I got married. So after over twenty years of marriage and what seemed like constant unrest, my prayer was answered. No more fighting!

In the meantime, while my parents remained together as my brother and I grew up, we endured life as we knew it. I was blessed to be exposed to healthy family dynamics, whether it be through the close-knit family of my best friend who happened to be from a conservative Mormon family with strong values, or a shining example set before me through an aunt and uncle. I knew that our family was not normal, and I desired something different.

Chapter 2

Divine Appointments

Fast-forwarding through my life, hitting on the points that would ultimately puzzle piece themselves together into the culmination of my future son's healing, I arrived as a twelve year old from Southern California in the city of Louisville, Kentucky.

My family landed here after a couple of recent moves within our home state of California. What had appeared to be a lavish financial existence had ended with the bank taking back our home, and many other family belongings were repossessed. Unknown to me, we had never actually owned them. It was the summer before my eighth grade year when due to my dad's employer's California location being shut down, he was transferred to another location instead of being let go. We arrived in our new hometown. We were moving for the first time from a home into an apartment. It was quite an adjustment. Up until this point, all I had ever known was living in homes that were fashionably furnished, playing in well kept yards with well-known neighborhood kids. My mom had stayed at home to care for my brother and me, and occasionally took on the job of looking after neighbor children as well, or helping out with our school to help make ends meet. I had taken all that for granted. I hadn't known any different. Now I did.

In our new home, there was no furniture. My brother and I still had our bedroom pieces, and my parents had a bed, etc., but our couches and coffee table – all of our "family" furniture had been repossessed before we left California. A truck came one day and took the downstairs furniture out of our house. No one said much about it. The family living area of our apartment now sat largely empty. There was no yard, no one we knew to play with and a lot of newness all around me. There were basketball and tennis courts at the apartment complex, neither of which I had played before. Other than that, there was a small grassy area in front of our apartment building and just down the road a neighborhood with houses not unlike the ones I had once occupied. I now yearned for a home like those.

I had never been to a place like Louisville. Lush trees lined the winding roads on the rolling hills so thick that in places they seemed to bend themselves over the road until the foliage met above in a canopy-type fashion. The houses were all made of brick and they had basements. This in itself was a novelty. I had never seen a brick house in person before, and I certainly had never been in a basement. In California the homes were stucco with Mexican tile roofs. Things were different.

The move was hard on my brother and me. Since we didn't know anyone and the school year was yet to start, we spent our summer days together. We attempted to play tennis on the apartment complex's court. My brother, the supreme athlete, who had played on a tennis team before, quickly became frustrated with me. I had never played the sport at all. Trying as hard as I could to hit the ball, the majority of my swings cut through the air full power, only to somehow result in me turning the racquet last minute from leading with the wide target area designed to hit the ball, to the narrow rim outline of the racquet slicing through the air and completely missing the ball. After numerous attempts, I would finally make contact between the racquet and ball, only to hit the ball out of the entire court! After repeated increasingly passionate instruction from my brother on how to simply make the racquet and ball gracefully connect and travel over the net within the confines of the court, my brother was infuriated with me. His sixth grade temper got the best of him. "You are doing it on purpose! Just hit the ball inside the court!" he yelled.

"I'm trying! I think I am just too powerful." I think after one day, we decided to move on from tennis. It was no fun when only one person was hitting the ball.

Thankful to get out of the suffocating humidity we were now experiencing anytime we went outside, we decided to spend our time inside. We came up with a game of throwing a small rubber ball against a wall in our sparsely furnished apartment. When we grew tired of this, we would venture out into the heat taking walks to the area pet shop to look in on the kittens and other pets. We loved this pet shop. Previous to our move we had owned many different cats over the years, but we hadn't been able to take our cat with us to our apartment. The pet shop never got old. We would see all the new kittens brought in and see them grow from week to week and slowly be adopted out. We knew we couldn't have a cat at our apartment, so we started hoping for one of the many other pets we saw there: gerbils, mice, rats, etc. As an adult, I now see why my parents didn't agree to get us one of these animals.

Soon we anticipated starting school in our new city where we could meet other kids. Weeks before school started, my mom went to inquire about the sports and activities my brother and I would have a chance to participate in. It was here that my mom found out about the middle school's cheerleading team and their tryouts that would start shortly after school started. It was recommended to her that in preparation for tryouts I attend tumbling classes at an area cheerleading gym called Gym Tyme. My mom located the gym and enrolled me in classes. I loved them.

School soon started. More newness. My eyes were now opened to the existence of a world other than the one I had previously known. All the schools I had ever attended consisted of an outdoor campus. Schools here were different as the entire school was under one roof due to winter weather. I had never imagined such a thing. The kids were very different as well. I was decked out in the California fashion that had been popular back home, brands like Quicksilver and other surf wear. Not only was I new to town, but my clothing advertised it. Kids at my new school had L. L. Bean backpacks and wore shirts that said, "Climb Every Mountain." The girls whom I had classes with were primarily soccer players. I had only played soccer one year in my life as a kindergartner, and I had never played since because I hated it.

I never adjusted to the new group of kids, and from here on out my family never again had the finances to be on the up and up with any area fashion trends. This was a little hard to take, moving into a time in childhood where this becomes an especially important factor in determining one's social status at school. My mom had done her research, and we were enrolled in the wealthiest and most affluent school district in Louisville, so we would have the best schooling and best teachers. But we didn't have the money, clothes or home that was up to par with our new peers.

In Louisville, middle school included grades 6 through 8. By the eighth grade, the year we moved to Louisville, most students at the middle school had already formed their cliques and groups of friends. Because I was not one to easily meet new people or even talk to someone who did not initiate a conversation with me, I failed to form a bond with anyone. After an unfulfilling year at my middle school, I decided that instead of attending the local high school, applying to the area's magnet high school, du Pont Manual, wouldn't be a bad idea. The high school, Manual, was combined with one of the nation's Youth Performing Arts Schools known as YPAS. YPAS specialized in training students in a specific performing art, dance, theater, musical theater, vocal music, instrumental music, design and production or piano. My mom had recommended that I apply to YPAS and audition for the Theater or Dance Department. Joining a new group of kids and pursuing new opportunities seemed like a good idea at this point to me.

With very little experience and even less known self-interest in the art, I decided to apply for the Theater Department. If accepted to YPAS, I would take my academic classes at du Pont Manual and walk a short distance later in the day to the YPAS Building to take acting and theater classes.

After getting accepted to YPAS, I again was about to enter another school where I would not know anyone. I didn't think there was one person from my current middle school who would be attending my new high school with me. I continued attending the local cheer gym where not only was I working on my tumbling skills, but I was meeting girls who had the same interests as me. The cheer gym was located across town in a warehouse-type environment. I would soon learn that Louisville, Kentucky, is the cheerleading capital of the world, and the owner of the gym I was attending was the head honcho of all things cheer. He was still revolutionizing the sport. Under his direction, I excelled at tumbling and learning new skills like stunting and basket tosses. I soon discovered that this "head honcho," James Speed, the owner of the gym, was also the coach of the magnet school I would soon be attending. After learning this, with his encouragement, I decided I would try out to cheer for my new high school.

The cheerleading program at du Pont Manual was one of the most successful in the country, so I was ecstatic when I, along with several other freshmen, made the varsity team. There were four of us in particular who were quickly designated "best friends." I say we were best friends, but really it was by default. Two of the best friends really were that. They had grown up through elementary and middle school together and had been close for a long time. These two "best friends" explained to us (I and the other girl) that we had to be "best friends," due to the fact that we were left over. They always said it jokingly, but we also knew it was true. Nonetheless, my friend and I shared a true bond and a great friendship that grew for a good year. We would practice our cheerleading skills at one another's homes, goof off in biology and spend time with the other half of our foursome.

However, as time progressed, it was apparent that the culture that existed between the four of us is what I would describe as the "mean girl crowd." No, nothing horrible ever happened to me hanging out with these girls, and in fact to this day I have a genuine affection for each of them. It is just that I should have never been a part of this social circle. These were not the type of girls I would be naturally drawn to, or them to me, left to our own devices. I was noticeably unconfident, unsure of myself, quiet and innocent. I remember my drama teacher constantly riding me to stop apologizing for myself. He said by my actions I was continually telling people, "Sorry."

He was right. I never wanted to be noticed, never cause a problem and never draw attention to myself. I quickly realized that I hated acting.

My new friends were the exact opposite. They were outwardly confident, outgoing, aggressive and at times abrasive. I didn't know how to react to the hurtful interaction that was commonplace among the girls. In the past, while growing up in California, I had always fit in with friends who were smart, funny, and cute and who had been raised with the same morals and often religious views as me. Remember, my previous best friend had been from a strong Mormon family, and I had been pretty sheltered in my interaction with my peers. This was my first experience with the "it" girls or the lead social crowd, and somehow I was in it, even if by default. However, my current situation was complicated by the fact that my friendships and the crowd I was now a part of had nothing to do with shared values. Our friendship was predicated solely on the fact that we cheered Varsity together, and thus we were now designated into a particular social group.

I loved cheering. It was my thing. The gym was my place. It was a great time for me. James demanded more from me than anyone ever had. Yet he also let me know that he cared about us as people. On the flip side, the more I learned about the new girls I cheered with, the more out of place I felt when I was with them outside of the gym. After our first squad sleepover, I was scared. I felt guilty and nervous around the girls. After revelations from the slumber party, I thought, Oh no, these are bad girls. Adding to that fact was that our team was so close. We practiced together and hung out together. I would say that this is pretty typical of most successful teams. Our bond was great.

What was not typical (I didn't know this until years later) is that because our coach rewarded members by skill and not seniority, our Varsity squad had freshmen like myself, right out of the eighth grade, who had never kissed a boy, never drank alcohol, never smoked or experimented with any drugs suddenly forced into the social circle of juniors and seniors who regularly had sex, smoked pot, and did things I had never even heard of. They expected to see the new freshmen girls initiated into the same scene. My group of four best friends seemed more than anxious and willing for all the new experiences to come, but I was scared.

You may be wondering how my family move as a middle schooler or my association with my new group of friends has anything to do the future healing of my son. You must remember that God knows the end from the beginning. Even though He was far from my thoughts at this point in my life, He had not forgotten me. Without my knowledge, He led and guided me right where I was at, using who I was with. God was faithful to me.

The four of us "best friends" cheered together our freshman and sophomore years, but by my junior year we had grown apart and went in different directions. Only two of us were on the same squad at this point, and we weren't much more than acquaintances. Cheerleading was such a dominant sport at our school that there were two different Varsity cheerleading squads. The "Red" squad was more competitive while the "White" squad was not as intense. As my former "best friends" and I had gone our separate ways socially and became more distanced, two hard workers were promoted from the "White" team to the "Red" team my junior year.

This was the point where I really "found" friends of my own, friends who were not only on the same squad as me, but with whom I also shared some life values. One of these girls was Julie Dunn. When I met Julie she was a hardworking, super petite Kate Moss-esque, blonde haired beauty. Julie didn't make the "Red" Varsity squad until her sophomore year, my junior year. (She was one year younger than me.) As a freshman she had entered the cheer program literally around 75 lbs., about 5'1" and was extremely awkward. Like me, she was quiet and innocent. During that first year she and her friend Lindsay, a quiet and reserved sweet brunette, worked tirelessly to conquer the skills needed to make the Red competitive squad for their sophomore year. When both Julie and Lindsay made the squad, we were almost instantly friends. Both girls were goal-oriented and extremely hardworking. We spent a lot of time together perfecting our stunting skills, and the task at hand brought us closer.

Julie and I were especially determined to be the best at our particular positions. Both Julie and Lindsay were very sweet and believed in God and allowed Him to have a role in their lives. This is not to say that we remained angels throughout high school or escaped uncorrupted by any means. Simply put, I believe we were initially drawn to each other, because we recognized our common values and beliefs in addition to our love of cheer.

By the time we were nearing the completion of high school, we had defiantly evolved from the innocent girls we initially were, but we still held the truth in our hearts. It was through the open door of this friendship, the summer before my senior year in high school, that divine appointments had been lined up in my life.

Lindsay invited me to go on a spiritual Christian retreat called Chrysalis, which made an impact on her life and mine. Looking back, I am a little surprised that she invited me and that I attended. She was closer to Julie than me, yet I was the one invited. Also, I didn't know anyone on the retreat. I wasn't a part of any church and I didn't know anyone putting the retreat on, but I went anyway and it did something to me.

After a fun-filled extended weekend full of study, worship, bonding activities and prayer, we came to the last day of Chrysalis. Following an intense worship session, we headed back to our designated rooms in mandated silence for a time to reflect. Upon entering my room, I saw a paper bag festively decorated on one side with the words "Chrysalis 21" and "Here I am, Lord" on the other. The bag was lying on my bed. It was filled to the brim. It was a most unexpected gift. Dumping out the contents of the bag, I discovered dozens of handwritten letters from friends, family and people whose lives I had impacted. They had taken the time to write what my life meant to them, that I was loved, special and that they had been praying specifically for me throughout this weekend. These letters made a huge impact on me. I had always known that I was loved, but it was still an overwhelming experience to be bombarded with an expression of love so intimately, by so many, at the same time.

I didn't even know how these letters had arrived. Obviously, someone had spent a great deal of time organizing the whole thing. There were letters from family members who lived on the other side of the country that I had not seen in years, from teachers, friends and camp counselors. I was crying as I read them realizing how loved and cared about I was. To this day I still have that bag filled with those letters.

Looking back, Chrysalis was an event that made a major impact on my life, allowing God to direct my path. What a good and faithful God! I don't recall asking for direction, yet now I could see how He was providing it.

I had come to that all-important time in my life, choosing college. I always knew I would go to college. School always came reasonably easy to me, and I had great aspirations of a successful career. At this point I had decided that I wanted to pursue a career in Broadcast Journalism. It seemed almost everyone from our high school would be attending the University of Kentucky. I didn't want to go to a school where everyone I knew was though. I had never really fit in with everyone from high school.

Because the University of Kentucky did not offer a

degree in my major, it was ruled out. I knew I wanted to go away to school, but still I had no idea where.

About the time I began to really ponder my options, my Uncle Michael, about five years older than me, arranged to drive me cross-country for some purpose that to this day I cannot remember. Michael is the youngest of my mom's seven siblings and the only boy. He is tall and slender with blue green eyes, blond hair and a sincere, thoughtful demeanor. Michael had always attended private Christian schools and excelled not only in his schooling, but he was also upheld for his high moral integrity. He had great expectations and aspirations for his life that we all knew he would achieve. I respected my uncle. I am almost positive that my Grandma Alice had been one of the masterminds who had arranged for Michael to drive with me and speak with me, but anyway Uncle Michael took this trip as an opportunity to seriously speak into my life.

The chaos of my parents' relationship was no secret to my relatives, and I am glad that Michael took it upon himself to provide direction in my life when I really needed it. Michael told me about how I was entering into a time in my life where the decisions I made now and throughout the next ten years would affect the entire course of my life. He was right. It was an eye-opening discussion. He explained that where I went to college would probably help determine who I would marry, as most people meet their future spouse at college, and it would even influence the career I would enter into and where I would live. This one decision would shape much of my future. By the end of our conversation, I was fully convinced by all the points that he brought up that this decision was one I needed to take very seriously.

Michael's mother, my Grandma Alice, had been encouraging me to check out a Christian school in the state called Asbury. I never looked into the school. From the pamphlets and materials my grandma sent me, it seemed small and wasn't appealing to me. However, on the heels of my conversation with Michael, my Aunt Karen and Uncle Clint, whom I had the utmost respect and admiration for based on the solidity of their marriage and family, made a point to talk to me about attending Oral Roberts University, a Christian University that they themselves had attended.

Unknown to me at that time, Oral Roberts was an actual person – a man who had a thriving healing ministry that began around the 1950's. His ministry functioned through "revivals" and "tent crusades." Mr. Roberts later went on to found the University. He was called by God to raise up a generation of students "to hear My voice, to go where My light is dim, where My voice is heard small, and My healing power is not known, even to the uttermost bounds of the earth. Their work will exceed yours, and in this I am well pleased." The focus of the University was to educate the whole person – spirit, mind and body.

I had never heard of the school nor did I know that several of my aunts and uncles had also attended the college. But the fact that my Aunt Karen and Uncle Clint were alumni and endorsed the school made a huge impact on me. Karen and Clint had what I would describe as the model family. They had met each other while attending O.R.U. and had created a Christ- centered family that consisted of three boys and a girl. Their standards for their family were high and I loved that. Their faith was tried and true. I had known that their firstborn son had faced life-threatening medical difficulties. Relying on God through their trials and tribulations, they had grown in their walk with the Lord as a result of it, and their son and family are thriving today. They were real and they lived their Christianity out more than any family I had ever been exposed to. After talking with them, I was convinced to go ahead and schedule a visit to O.R.U. during "college weekend." If I decided I didn't like it, I simply wouldn't go. Plus, the University offered my major! What more could I want?

So I boarded a plane and flew from Louisville, Kentucky, to Tulsa, Oklahoma. My Uncle Clint's parents, whom I had never met, Kay and Charles Taylor, had arranged to pick me up from the airport. They helped me get my bags and loaded them into their car. Although this was my first time meeting Kay and Charles, I immediately loved them. Kay looked to be in her fifties and her natural beauty was enhanced by the joy she radiated. Charles was of similar age, tall, slender in build and warm, but reserved. They carried themselves with an air of confidence, and I knew they must be highly esteemed within their community.

During the ride to their home from the airport, the Taylors told me about how both of their kids had attended O.R.U. and how they had eventually followed their children from their hometown in Texas to Oklahoma. Before we arrived at their home, Charles made a quick detour and drove by the campus to show me the dorms and where I would be dropped off in the morning. I was shocked as they showed me what I was told were famed praying hands on the campus. The sculptures made in the shape of two hands raised together in prayer were a sight to see. Standing 60 feet tall and weighing 30 tons, they were made of bronze and surrounded by flags representing the various countries of the University's diverse student population. I also could see the University's Prayer Tower from afar. The top of it was lit by a natural gas fed flame that burns continuously, reminding us that there are always people praying. I had never known that any of this had even existed. What was this place? Clearly this was not a typical college.

We pulled away from the campus and continued on toward the Taylor's home. I was informed that if I ever needed anything, they would be right there. They lived only about fifteen minutes from the campus. As we approached their home, we entered into a gated community. Right away my attention was turned toward the awe-inspiring surroundings. Beautiful brick and stone homes, with lush green rolling hills lining the streets. The homes were set back behind large trees. They came in a variety, strong and sturdy or gracefully, artfully swooping. I was mesmerized by the neighborhood. Wow! This is where they lived! As we pulled in the drive Charles informed me, "You know our daughter Charla lives next door. You will have to meet her sometime."

By the time we arrived it was late. As I entered through the garage and into the kitchen, I took in the beauty of their home and its décor. The home had worn wood floors that had been painted in a large black and white checked pattern. The open kitchen was painted in warm yellow tones. It felt eclectic in its decor, artistic and upscale.

I remember examining my room upon my entrance and being amazed that there was actual fabric on the walls. Not wallpaper, but fabric. I decided right then and there that at some point I would like to have a room with fabric on the walls. (This has yet to happen in my life, but I have now been reminded.) Also, chocolates filled the decorative glass container on the desk in my room, another detail that girls are quick to take note of. I quickly got ready for bed, just as excited about the next day as I was about this room.

The next morning I awoke early and loaded my luggage into the car with Charles. He drove me to the campus and dropped me off where the "weekenders" signed in. Now that I was seeing the campus in the daylight, I was struck at how different it was. Hues of gold and blue adorned the majority of the campus. It was modern in a retro 70's sort of way. But what really stood out to me about the University, then and still today, is the people.

Up until this point in my life, other than with my best friends in elementary school that I had moved away from, I had never felt the kind of acceptance from my peers that I felt during that weekend. After checking in for the weekend, we were put in groups. We stayed in the dorms in rooms with current students we had never met before, on the same floor as other "weekenders" in our group. Everyone was loving and welcoming. Students attending the University were not just from the surrounding area, groups of friends that had known each other throughout high school like you would expect to find at many state universities. At O.R.U., the majority of the student body was made up of individuals who had traveled across the country to attend a school where they could learn while at the same time be surrounded by teachers and other students who were all trying to submit to God's will in their lives. It was truly an amazing experience that built upon what was introduced to me during the Chrysalis weekend in high school. God was continuing to silently guide me on a specific path in a seemingly self-directed life.

One thing that amazed me about the students I met during my visit was how normal they were. They were not geeky or socially awkward, like I might have imagined before attending the weekend. They were normal high school kids. That really surprised me. I was put in an orientation group with a high school homecoming queen and an overly flirtatious brunette among others. There were as many different personalities represented throughout that weekend that are present in any school setting. The only thing unique about all the students was the fact that we all passionately shared the same core beliefs. We all had the same foundational truth to build on – we believed in Jesus as Lord and Savior. That was our common denominator.

We attended a school-wide chapel service, just like we would be required to attend biweekly upon enrolling in the University. The praise and worship were amazing. I was blown away. All of these kids were singing their hearts out and seeking God. As this went on, one of the girls who was a host during the weekend quietly pulled me aside and said, "God wants me to tell you that He loves you." I didn't know what to say to her. I had never experienced anything like that before with God saying something personal to me. I just lost it. Then and there in the chapel service I began bawling. The God of the universe said that to me! He loves me! It was too much. But it was just what I needed and He knew it.

Later, I wanted to find the girl and quiz her: "Did you hear His voice? How did you know it was God? What exactly did He say?" From that weekend on, it was decided that I would be going to O.R.U. and I was so excited to get there!

Chapter 3

Another World

My plane landed and I entered into a fog of summer humidity. The heat smothers all of Oklahoma during late August, which was when I arrived to begin my freshman semester. Gratefully I quickly located and boarded the campus shuttle from the airport and headed toward what would soon be my new home. There were only a couple of other students on the shuttle with me. We were a rarity among the new freshmen being ushered onto the campus that day. The majority of new students were being dropped off and unpacked by their parents.

The shuttle pulled into the lower lot on campus, a location central to all the campus dormitories. As I made my way out of the shuttle and parking lot, I was greeted at once by hundreds of new faces busily walking purposefully in all directions. Quickly, I joined the mass commute, walking with the new students (returning students arrived at a later date). Almost all of the new students had their parents accompany them, along with what I thought was an exorbitant amount of material possessions for attending college.

As I exited the parking lot, I headed toward my dormitory. My dorm was located just across from the campus cafeteria and was backed up to the prayer gardens. The gardens consisted mainly of some plants and flowers planted amidst fountains, pools of water and darting concrete walkways that broke off from each other in symmetrical and angular fashion. These walkways ultimately led to the main building, the "GC" where classes were held. I reached the dormitory and entered an elevator packed with incoming students and their mothers who were carrying an endless supply of their daughters' personal possessions. Getting off on the fourth floor, I located my room – the last room on the left at the end of the hall. Carrying my two suitcases, I entered the empty room, dropped off my bags and headed down to complete the tedious registration process, finalize student loan paperwork and pick up my schedule.

As I exited the dorm and headed toward the GC, I couldn't help but notice that everywhere I looked there were families waiting in the long lines together, making sure meal plans were correct, bags were unpacked and dorm rooms decorated. I was there on my own. I know if my parents could have afforded to make the trip, they would have been there in a heartbeat. It just wasn't financially possible. As for me, I couldn't have been happier. I wouldn't have wanted it any other way. I am a very independent person, and this was going to be me making my way in my new life the way I wanted it. I was filled with anticipation and excitement.

It wasn't long until the families and the parents helping their sons and daughters settle in said their good-byes and headed home.

My new life began. Attending O.R.U. was very different from the reality I left. I loved it. I came from a home where there was no peace to a University that was committed to teaching its students to seek God and His purpose in their lives, which gives peace. There were many rules, but I didn't mind. I have never been a rule-breaker (even though to this day my husband swears my skirts were shorter than permitted by the school dress code; I certainly didn't intend it) and had always felt out of place with my high school friends as they pushed the limits of what I knew was right.

In order to attend O.R.U., there was an Honor Code that students were required to sign. Among other things we had to agree not to drink, smoke or engage in sexual activities outside of the context of marriage. There was a nightly curfew, same sex dorms and a dress code. Basically, there were standards. Instead of saying, "Anything goes," the University's stance was, "God wants the best for your life. We want to help you achieve that and through these mandated expectations we hope we will help keep you from veering off track." I loved this school. It was a loving place full of fun and acceptance. I would love to send all of my five children there one day if they desire to go there!

The thing about O.R.U. was it ignited a hunger in me. It was a catalyst, creating a desire in me that I never even knew I had. It introduced me to the supernatural.

There were biweekly mandatory school-wide chapel services consisting of nearly five thousand students, faculty and staff. We sat in assigned rows grouped by the floors of our dormitories, packed in with our closest friends. We sang praise and worship together, upbeat and emotion provoking songs as an enthusiastic and highly talented band and choir of our peers led us. We regularly heard preaching from some of the most respected charismatic preachers in the country. We were fed the Word of God from the Bible. I heard people praying and speaking in tongues, saw countless healings during special healing services and heard countless testimonies of students who had been touched during a specific service.

Did I ever receive the gift of speaking in tongues? That supernatural occurrence mentioned in the Bible at Pentecost when the Holy Spirit physically speaks through your mouth, using your voice, uttering in languages you do not know, nor have you learned. Did I ever receive a physical healing, either through receiving prayer and someone physically laying their hands on me requesting that God heal me, or through a spontaneous supernatural touch possibly while worshiping the Lord? No, but I wanted these things. My eyes had been opened to another world. I knew enough about God, about feeling His work in my life, feeling His love and peace to know that what I was experiencing was real, and now I just knew that I wanted more of it.

I would go out into the school's fields alone many times during those warm nights. The campus was park-like in many areas with green expanses of grass dotted with large trees and darting squirrels. I would walk the fields, look up at the stars and talk to God. I'd tell Him that I wanted that stuff, the Him stuff. I wanted to experience Him and I wanted to hear Him. Just like God is with you and me right now, wherever we may be and whatever we may be experiencing, God hears us. Though I didn't feel it at the time, God heard me then and He hears me now.

I think He must have been saying, "Listen and you will hear." He is still saying it. At the time, however, it wasn't loud enough for me. His voice wasn't what I expected it to be, so I failed to hear Him those nights in the field. I felt peace, joy and excitement that He loved me, He had a plan for me and He was there with me. All this I knew, but I heard no "voice." I desperately wanted to have a supernatural experience with Him.

One of the academic requirements of the University was a course called Charismatic Life and Ministry. The class basically taught all the cool stuff that prior to attending O.R.U. I had never been exposed to. These were things such as healings, speaking in tongues, visions, words of knowledge, etc. The class was structured in a biweekly format.

One day it was taught by a dull, seemingly lifeless professor in a very monotonous group lecture format, where he basically read out of a book to an auditorium full of students. I literally would have to shake myself to stay awake, and there would be small pockets of the nearly three hundred students packed into the lecture hall that would actually be bobbing their heads in and out of a semi-conscious sleep state regularly throughout the class.

The second class of the week was taught by the school's then president, the founder Oral Roberts' son, Richard Roberts. His teaching style differed greatly from that of the lecturing professor. Richard taught in an off-the-cuff sort of way. He presented the material confidently, enthusiastically, almost theatrically. With experienced stage presence, he would cover the topics in a highly involved sort of way. Teaching on healing, he wouldn't just talk about what the scriptures taught on healing, he would go on to actively pray and physically lay his hands on students who were in need of correcting specific physical ailments. The students would then publicly present their results from the prayers to the class from the "stage" and tell us what they experienced as they were touched and prayed over.

Some testified of full healings right there. Others felt they had experienced a warmth or some other sensation and that their healing had been initiated during the prayer. I am sure there were others who failed to notice any difference at all, but I wasn't focused on them.

Richard would go on to recount stories of previous miraculous healings that were fresh in his mind. He would also explain to us firsthand when he was receiving a word of knowledge. A word of knowledge is knowledge that is supernaturally revealed to someone from God that otherwise would be unknown.

"I'm hearing 'back.' Yes, 'back'! Did you hurt your back recently?" Richard would inquire of a singled-out student.

"Well, I think I strained the upper right part the other day and it has been sore ever since."

The "word" received during these healing sessions almost always contained specifically what body part someone needed healing for. Richard then would proceed to pray for the individual as the knowledge instructed.

As I remember, it was near the end of the semester in Richard's class after a teaching on the gift of "praying in the Spirit." (Praying in the Spirit, or in tongues, is when through the influence of the Holy Spirit, one begins speaking/praying in different languages and utterances, while their spirit is in communion with God.) Students who wanted to receive the gift were invited to receive prayer for it. The whole class was amazing and exciting to me. It was magical. I LOVED IT!

Once a week when Richard Roberts taught the class, it was held in an arena setting in the "Baby Mabee" Building, which was quite a trek from the main area of campus where all other classes were held. The "Baby Mabee" was where the Roberts' family filmed their television programs, and it adjoined the arena where the University's basketball games were held. Anyway, you really had to rush to the facility, because they locked the classroom doors on late arrivals. If you were like me and thought this was the most interesting stuff you had ever heard, you were moving as quickly as possible so that you could make it to the front row. Who knows? If I was in the front row, I might get hands laid on me, or have a healing or be the recipient of a word of knowledge! The point is, I valued being up front and because the seating was stadium-esque, if you were not down in front, you were high up, which was too far away from the action for my liking!

It was during this time of my college life that I had formed a friendship with a guy named Clay. Clay was unlike anyone I had ever met before or since. He was an in-shape, 6'1", blond-haired, blue-eyed athletic college guy like so many others. It was not his looks that differentiated him from everyone else. It was his personality. Clay was the most energetic, motivated, opinionated, friendly and charismatic guy I knew. We had class together before Charismatic Life and we had Charismatic Life together, so we would walk together to the class.

There was only one problem. Clay HATED Charismatic Life. He thought the whole thing was bogus, and specifically he thought Richard Roberts was bogus. He would purposely walk slow, dragging his feet to take as long as possible to get to class, making sure to moan and complain throughout the entire trip. He wanted to be the last one in. If we were a little early he would insist on standing outside of the door and entering right before they locked it so he could sit in the very back because he wanted to be as far from Richard Roberts as possible. It would infuriate me. This was my class!

Clay had a friend, Mark, who was also in our class and was really nice. He volunteered to drive a group of us to class every week so we always made it in good time. However, I recall that by the end of the semester, Clay's antics regularly kept us in the back of the nearly three hundred students who attended the class.

Chapter 4

Life Begins

Looking back, another great thing about O.R.U. was that it provided a great atmosphere to find quality guys to date. I had attended many "get your roommate a date" and some casual dates while at O.R.U. I can honestly say that every single guy I dated was nice and top-tier quality. You see, when you attend a school with moral standards, your success at finding a quality guy really increases!

Anyway, there was one guy in particular whom I had been dating. To this day, I will say that you could not find a nicer guy. Initially, I was attracted to him due to his good looks. He had piercing blue eyes and jet-black hair. I loved that he was athletic and played on the University soccer team. Many of the girls I knew found him attractive and very sweet. I really didn't know him well as I was extremely shy, and he was a reserved and quiet guy. Basically, we had no foundational base for a relationship. We just found the other attractive. Quickly we were labeled as "dating."

Almost everyone on my wing insisted that I would

marry him! They thought he was amazing! I remember listening to my Resident Advisor tell me about how we were so perfect for each other, and she was sure we would end up together as she had seen so many other girls get married after meeting their mate at college. This made me rather sad. I felt let down as to what love was "supposed" to feel like. All these girls thought we were perfect, and yet, I felt nothing for the guy. In fact, we hardly knew each other, and I was hard pressed to carry on a conversation with him when I had to. I don't think we ever even held hands. We definitely never kissed. Because I had no real "boyfriend dating relationship" experience, I had nothing to compare my current situation to. I just figured this is how it was. He certainly had all the right traits.

He was attractive. He was godly, which was awesome. I remembered being amazed as he told me about a vision he had had. I don't remember what the subject of the vision was or what its message was. I was just impressed that he had had one. He said the water in it reminded him of how light would reflect off of the sequins on a prom dress. I was amazed. In my mind he was some sort of superior spiritual being, but that was it. There was nothing more I felt for him. No connection.

"If this is as good as it gets, it certainly means I am destined to be single!" Luckily, the thought of living single wasn't upsetting to me in the least bit, as I knew the harsh reality of my parents' marriage. I certainly didn't want to get married unless I knew that is what/who God wanted for me. I took my non-existent feelings for my "boyfriend" as a reflection on myself and my fate meaning that surely I was never to get married. I must not be the marrying type. I accepted my fate and was fine with it, content to move on. Subconsciously I think what really did it in for me with this super nice, attractive guy was the fact that he wanted to be a schoolteacher. Although there is nothing wrong with schoolteachers, I believe I am attracted to someone who is more ambitious, somewhat risky, maybe even a little crazy in their goals for their life.

This guy must have been feeling the same thing as I felt; namely, nothing, because after Christmas break of my freshman year, he sat me down and he said he wasn't really "feelin' it." Actually I don't remember what was said, but the end result was that we were not together and we were both cool with it. Seriously, the relationship never went anywhere, but I think we can both attribute that to God's goodness, because the two of us together was definitely not meant to be.

The timing of the breakup was perfect though, because I was starting to get a little nervous. I mean, even though this "boyfriend" and I were no closer than two fifth graders going out, we still were dating, and at the same time, I suddenly realized that I was being pursued by my friend Clay, the Charismatic Life hating fanatic, and I kind of liked it too!

For the longest time, I didn't even know I was being pursued by Clay. He was so outgoing and friendly with everyone he met, I just thought we were friends. Thus far our relationship had consisted of one roommate date that

I had attributed to a coincidence of his roommate picking me out for Clay since Clay and I were friends. I now know that Clay had orchestrated the date.

We would sit together during Mass Media Communications where he would draw elaborate stadiums and cityscapes with my name intertwined all over my folders. We would walk or ride in Mark's car to Charismatic Life together with our friends. Then, Clay would meet up with me in the cafeteria where he loved to crash the table I sat at with my wing and harass my Chaplain and Resident Advisor. I think my Chaplain was starting to worry that he might not be a great guy for me to be friends with. He was continually debating the latest chapel sermon or honor code rule with her. He always brought a bit of humor to these encounters, but the results of the banter would still leave her genuinely upset. For some odd reason Clay enjoyed this.

Things changed with Clay right before we left for Christmas break my freshman year. Clay helped pay his way through school by working for a mobile entertainment company as a DJ for school dances, weddings, etc. He had invited me to go with him where he was a DJ for a company Christmas party somewhere off campus. I had been places with Clay before since he was one of the few on campus who had a vehicle. He would often drive my friend and me to the store, or a group of friends would go and get coffee or something together. But I had never been anywhere alone with Clay, nor had it ever crossed my mind. He was just a friendly, life of the party, big group, social kind of guy.

My friend Keri, who also knew Clay from Charismatic Life and from many other friendly group outings, hadn't made any plans for the evening that Clay had invited me out. Most other students had already left campus for Christmas break. Not knowing Clay had intentions to make me more than a friend, I thought I should invite our mutual friend to come along. I was still in the dorms due to cheerleading commitments, and Keri was staying behind working in the basketball team's PR Department. She, like me, had one more basketball game to attend before she could go home for the holiday break.

Clay was still in town, fulfilling his work commitments and serving as DJ for Christmas parties. Keri and I had become very close during the past semester, and she was also friends with Clay. She lived just across the hall from me, and she had taken Charismatic Life with Clay and me and was a part of the weekly car rides to the "Baby Mabee" for class. She had told me on numerous occasions that she was sure Clay liked her as he was always calling to hang out with us. I thought it made perfect sense for her to join Clay and me, and we could all go to his show together since usually we all hung out together anyway.

Keri was a cute, outgoing, very flirtatious petite blonde who thought just about every guy she met liked her. She might have been right, too, or maybe they just enjoyed flirting with an easy target. She loved to tell our group of girlfriends what specific guys did and said and how they were totally in love with her. She had been under the impression that Clay was one of the many young men interested in her, and she told me about it so much that I believed he liked her too.

Prior to the prevalence of personal cell phones, I had been unable to reach Clay on the phone in his dorm room to let him know Keri was coming to the DJ show with us. Anyway, Keri and I left the empty dorms together and ventured down to the lower parking lot where Clay was going to meet me. He was already there waiting. His cartoonish, brightly colored, hand-painted Ford Escort was ready with him holding the door open as he saw us coming.

"Keri is coming with us," I announced the obvious as we arrived together. "She is here until the basketball game too."

Keri and I climbed in the front seat and shared it together, smiling and laughing the whole time. The backseat and trunk were overloaded with all of the equipment needed for his mobile disc jockey performance. Clay pulled out and we left campus.

Clay said he had a couple of errands to run before we would head to his show. I don't recall specifically where we went on those errands, probably a short trip to Wal-Mart. Then, instead of heading out to the show, Clay surprisingly drove us back to the lower parking lot on campus where he had previously picked us up only a short time earlier. Once the car stopped, Clay told Keri that he was dropping her off, and we would continue on without her.

"Bye, Keri!" Clay stated. I'm not sure what kind of excuse he gave her about why she could not continue on with us, or even if he went to the effort to give her an excuse. I imagine he may have told her something to the effect that the client wouldn't have liked him bringing along all these "friends" to the show, and he only felt comfortable bringing one. That is why he had invited me, or maybe it was the space issue. We were pretty cramped as it was, but we weren't complaining. However, he didn't explain. Clay simply stated that Keri had to leave. She could not come to the show with us.

We sat for a second stunned. Did he really just tell Keri to leave? I couldn't believe it. Neither of us saw this coming. I thought Keri was going with us to the show!

"Vanessa will be back later," Clay announced.

Keri and I continued to process our shock for a moment. Then she opened the door and exited the vehicle. She stood looking at me in the car with a confused look on her face. Possibly she was wondering whether or not I would join her.

"Bye, Keri," I said as sweetly as possible. I hoped she wasn't mad. "I'll see you when I get back." I pulled the door shut, and Clay backed out and left while she was still standing in the parking lot amidst the cold winter air. Clay and I proceeded to have what I will classify as our first "real date."

I was comfortable with Clay. We joked and laughed as he drove his car across town to the Sheridan Hotel where the show would take place in one of the ballrooms. Unlike my relationship with my current soccer playing boyfriend, Clay and I genuinely had a friendship and were able to relate to one another. I attribute a significant portion of the creation of this successful friendship to Clay. It didn't come naturally to me, that's for sure.

To this day Clay recalls that previously on our room-mate date, I hardly spoke at all. I would smile, was pleas-ant and sweetly answered any questions he had, with concise one-word answers, but mostly I looked around nervously and didn't have a true conversation with him.

I failed to notice anything unusual about this date versus any others. This was how I normally acted around guys. I was not comfortable around them. I didn't know how to act around them, and I didn't know how they ex-pected me to interact with them. Clay must have seen this as a challenge because since that roommate date, he had regularly harassed me, teasing me and in any way engaging me until at last it was easy and comfortable for me to relate to him.

All the while I was dating the soccer player, under the presumption of Clay being my friend, he walked with me to class, wrote me funny poems, drew silly drawings for me, called me by various ever-changing nicknames (Miss orange pants, swan, big shooter, etc.). He would intentionally single me out and embarrass me. I think he enjoyed making me blush.

In our classes together, Clay always sat by me as I took notes and he drew. We began studying together after classes. We would meet at a designated common area on the bottom of his dorm. It was primarily empty as most students found more exciting areas to hang out together. It was a sparsely decorated carpeted space equipped with a small kitchen area, a television and a random assortment of seating. Clay would bring his blender and make smoothies for us. Then we would proceed to study for whatever the most impending test was on the horizon in our many classes together. I specifically remember having to memorize scripture for Old Testament for eight hours straight with him. I am not joking. Clay had a very hard time memorizing things. He was an extremely hard worker and would insist that we not stop until it was all learned. I would have preferred that we study a little bit at a time, take a break and come back to the task at hand, but that was not how Clay operated. We could not stop until the whole thing was done and we would study the entire time. Of course, with Clay's off-the-wall dynamic personality, the studying couldn't help but be fun and entertaining. Clay would make up dirty or silly acronyms or songs to help him remember which scriptures were identified by which specific book, chapter and verse in the Bible.

Anyway, as a result of our intense interaction, teasing and harassment, I had become familiar and comfortable around Clay. As we headed off together to the Sheridan Hotel, there could not have been another person in the world I would have felt more at ease with and glad to be around.

We arrived at one the Sheridan Hotel ballrooms

where Clay instructed me on how to help him set up for the show. Soon after everything was in place, the event began. Clay hosted the Christmas party and went on to play music for the attendees throughout the night. It was fun to see him at his job. As the party came to a close and everyone had left, I went to turn on the lights and unplug the speakers to help Clay begin the task of taking down his equipment. As I walked back to the booth, it became apparent that Clay had plugged the speakers back in. He had a slow song playing, and he led me out on the floor to dance with him. Immediately, all ease and comfort I had felt with Clay were removed. Suddenly I was unsure of myself and what was going on. I wasn't sure what to think, but I liked it. We danced together as the music played. The dynamic between us had suddenly changed.

After the show we returned to campus right before curfew. As Clay pulled into the lower lot to drop me off, he opened his glove compartment and pulled out a badly wrapped gift that he had made me. Accompanying it was an intricate handmade card. Clay had personalized the card and artwork on it for me. It had obviously taken quite a bit of time, and it was brightly colored like his car and personality. I proceeded to open the wrapped gift. It was a funny CD consisting of a random mix of dance and Christmas music. He had made this too, a fitting gift from a guy who was working as a DJ to pay his way through college.

The next day I left school to go home for Christmas break. All during break I thought about Clay, examined my card and listened to the CD he had made. We never had exchanged numbers and Facebook didn't exist at the time, so we had no contact over break.

As soon as we returned for the new semester after Christmas break, my current boyfriend and I broke up, and Clay and I officially began dating. Clay started pursuing me with laser beam focus. I will spare you all the details and make a long story short, but by the third time we went out I KNEW I was going to marry Clay. I think that says a lot because not much earlier I thought I would never marry and now I had no doubt. Now I knew that I knew that I knew I would marry Clay though I never said anything to him about it.

Clay proposed the summer after our freshman year at the University. Though I had known I would end up married to Clay, I never had anticipated on it being now. I excitedly accepted Clay's proposal, but we had a bit of disagreement about the timeline. Clay had assumed we would get married as soon as possible. I had never imagined being married during school. I had thought we should graduate school (three more years), live on our own for a bit and then get married. Clay thought this was the most ridiculous idea. Throughout the first semester following our recent engagement, Clay and I would regularly walk the campus and talk about our impending marriage. He had a goal in mind. "You know you want to marry me. Right?"

"Yes!" I replied. I was 100 percent sure.

"So why would you want to wait then?" he would inquire.

"Well, I need to finish school."

"Are you afraid if you get married you won't finish school?"

"No, I know I will finish school. I just always thought I would need to finish school and then live by myself for a while. You know, be independent."

Clay thought for a bit. "Is that what you always wanted to do? Or is that what people have told you to do?" Clay challenged.

Now it was my turn to think. "I guess that is what I have always been told I should do. Go to school, get a job, live on my own for a bit, then get married."

"But what do you want to do?"

"Well, I want to marry you."

"Then we should get married. It doesn't matter what anyone else thinks we should do. And at the end of our lives, we will have had those years together that we wouldn't have if we had waited." After several of these discussions, I came around to Clay's point of view.

So it was determined that Clay and I would get married following that school year, one week after I turned twenty. That was the way Clay lived his life. He didn't care what others thought. He made his decisions based on what he wanted, and once he knew what he wanted he pursued it. He was a go-getter.

Clay and I married the summer after our sophomore

year at O.R.U. Honestly, I am so glad that we did not wait and that we married when we did. It was the right decision for us. I loved being married and poured myself into it. I had long ago determined that if I ever got married I would have the best marriage possible and be the best wife I could be. I wanted to create the family I never had growing up. Clay poured himself into our marriage with the same passion.

Life was good. I continued to attend O.R.U., but I was so in love my head was elsewhere. I wanted to play this game called school and get through my classes as quickly as possible so I could graduate and focus even more on creating this new life together with my husband. I felt disconnected from the other students now that I was married. I felt like I was a part of another world. My life had begun and they were still determining what they wanted to do with theirs. I felt like an old soul around a bunch of kids.

Married life was wonderful. My husband was wonderful. We spent our newly married life getting accustomed to our roles as a married couple, going to school, working various odd jobs and planning. We loved planning what our lives would be like – how we would grow the DJ business, where we would travel, how we would reach our goals. It felt like we were invincible, that together we could conquer the world!

We attended a local church together called Believers. We had attended the church together when dating and the Interim Pastor, David Grothe (the church was in the process of finding a new pastor), had done our premarital counseling and married us. Believers was a fast growing church with many college-aged and young family members. The church met at a high school auditorium, since it did not have its own building yet. The praise and worship style and the church's overall energy were pretty much spot on to what we had experienced at O.R.U. We both enjoyed hearing David Grothe speak each week, and we knew many of the other church members from O.R.U.

Soon an official pastor was selected for the church. However, David Grothe was not selected as we had assumed and hoped he would be. Clay and I had a hard time transitioning to the new pastor. We stuck it out for a little while, but soon we stopped attending.

As a young married couple, we knew we should be in church. I felt convicted to attend and in addition, it was mandated as part of the Honor Code to attend a local church while a student at O.R.U. We visited different area churches and congregations during this time, but we never clicked with any of them. Clay was an especially hard shoe to fit in this as he didn't completely believe in God at the time, so he regularly took issue with what the pastors were saying at the various churches that we tried.

Over the years, we pretty much just settled in to not going, or randomly we would attend Carlton Pearson's church, Higher Dimensions. Carlton Pearson was a familiar face to those in the church circles of Tulsa, Oklahoma. An O.R.U. alumnus and a one- time close friend and protégé of the University's founder, Oral Roberts,

Carlton had started and grown his own church. Carlton was a black man with a very distinctive, flamboyant style. My husband was always amazed by the fashion ensembles that Carlton pulled off. A solid purple shirt that fit similar to a woman's blouse and was embellished by a swooping line of silver/gold glitter that from afar might be mistaken for a silver/gold chain that hung askew impossibly and unnaturally to one side, unlike a necklace which would have hung symmetrically. Clay loved this church. He loved the energy, the style and the presentation. The church was predominantly African-American, which was reflected in everything from the music choices and the way the songs were sung, to the fiery, theatrical presentation of the week's message by Carlton. Even though we enjoyed the services, we never actually became members, as there was a bit of controversy surrounding Carlton.

In recent years, Carlton had changed his views from that of a traditional Christian to embracing what he called the Gospel of Inclusion, which to me looked at lot like Universalism, meaning there would be parts of the Bible he didn't believe anymore. Even though we never became members, we did attend a lot. It was the one church Clay enjoyed.

Life continued on and it got a little crazy. I graduated from O.R.U., and we built our first home together. The house was completed just about the time I graduated. This was our dream home. I couldn't believe it. I was just barely out of college and here we were moving into a custom home that we had built, complete with wood floors and granite countertops. I was blessed to be married to a man who was passionate, loving and yes, ambitious. There was a reason the teacher friend had never worked out. Looking back, I would say that every area of our life was ideal, except for my husband's work schedule. It was extreme to say the least.

Beginning from DJ-ing to pay his way through college, Clay eventually left college. (He actually was forced to leave O.R.U. only a few short months before we were to be married.) He had started his own mobile entertainment company. As ambitious as he was, he worked tirelessly to grow it. Within a few short years, it would become the nation's largest non-franchised mobile entertainment company. In the beginning, as crazy as his work schedule was, between classes, an internship, a job and starting our own company, it was still manageable for us, because I worked with Clay on the business and thus we were able to spend time being together while being productive together.

After an eye-opening internship of my own at a local television news station, I had determined there was no way I would pursue Broadcast Journalism, the occupation I had obtained my degree in. My internship at the news station revealed to me that the career was in conflict with the ideal marriage and family life that I was on a mission to create for myself and my family. So I joined Clay in helping grow the entertainment business, and I coached cheerleading on the side.

Clay and I were almost always together. I wanted to

help him in any way possible, whether that was to accompany him as he DJ-ed a wedding, helping him create custom music mixes for clients or staying up all hours of the night helping assemble new gear or design advertisements. We were a great team.

However, after a little more than three years of marriage, our first child was born, Havana. She was wonderful. I loved being a mom. I felt like being a wife and a mom was what I was born to do, but as the majority of my time was spent taking care of her, I was no longer able to accommodate Clay's intense work schedule as easily. To complicate matters, business was booming, forcing us to move into a larger home only one year after we had moved into our current new home.

At this point, the business was run out of our home as Clay didn't see how it was possible to afford office space, even though he had never checked out lease rates. The more pressing problem was that my husband had not yet learned how to delegate and was literally working from about 5 a.m. to around 7 p.m. on a good night. Weekends were a disaster as far as meeting a spouse's need for quality time. As the business peaked, Clay worked every Friday during the day and Friday night until about 1:30 or 2:00 a.m. He worked all day Saturday, and Saturday night until around 4:00 a.m. On Sundays, he would pass out and sleep, understandably exhausted.

It was obvious that our lifestyle was not sustainable and would not be conducive to the family life I envisioned creating. The reality was and is that Clay and I have always had an extremely strong relationship. We have been blessed in this area and as things became harder, we would press in together to form a new plan. However, that plan always consisted of our own efforts and failed to ever involve us turning to God for His help.

More and more, I began to hand over my concerns to the Lord in prayer, as I wasn't able to make inroads with my husband about these issues. I have never wanted to be a nagging wife, and at the time my husband was unable to see the validity of my concerns or a way to satisfy them upon admitting that they may in fact hold some weight.

I was beginning to feel that the Lord might be intentionally allowing us to be put into more and more trying circumstances to force us to turn to Him. Specifically, I believed all this was possibly being orchestrated in order to change Clay's beliefs as I had continually prayed that he would come to know the Lord.

Much was going on all around us that only added to the stress of Clay's growing schedule – a new business partner who was not holding up his end of the deal with a new company; the large home that we had purchased unknown to us had major foundation problems that made selling it prohibitive; and of course our business bursting at the seams and needing a viable location. I didn't want to have to endure any worse scenarios, so I was on my knees praying by this time for some sort of relief that would result in Clay's schedule easing up.

I would also plead my case to my husband and inquire about us seeking the Lord's guidance together. He was infuriated at the idea. He did not believe God would or could do anything to help. It was up to him to figure it all out, he would declare. We never argued about this point, but I was really sympathetic towards my husband on it. He was under so much pressure believing he had to do it all on his own. His feelings were valid.

I actually hated it when friends or family members would debate with him about the goodness of God or God's role in our lives. Didn't they understand that arguing, debating and disagreeing would never change his or anyone's viewpoint on the issue? Only God could do that.

Clay had clearly explained to me that he genuinely wanted to believe that God was good. He desired to believe that God would intervene in people's lives in gracious, loving ways, but he simply could not will himself to believe something that in his heart he did not think was true. He was right. That is why we never argued about it. How can you demand someone to believe something? People either believe or they do not. Belief is not an argument to be won; rather a matter of the heart. So I prayed that Clay would believe and that God would show him the truth.

It may have been accurate that God was allowing our circumstances to compile and compound into a humanly insurmountable mountain. Adding to an already insane schedule, we were now in the process of trying to transition out of the failing business partnership which was complicated by the fact that the new entity created by this partnership had already acquired another company complete with debt that needed to be serviced. This brought on an even more unbelievable workload on my husband. He was trying to keep this new business afloat that the partnership now owned, making all the loan payments himself, while at the same time trying to dissolve the partnership and simultaneously continuing to run our entertainment company. It really was miserable. I prayed for it to end, for the whole thing to be over. Looking back, I am grateful that God took us to that point. Otherwise, my husband might not have desired to be done with this phase of running his love, the mobile entertainment company.

We were literally at the end of our rope. I couldn't complain though. How dare I complain to my husband that I wasn't seeing him. He would have LOVED to be done with work and get to see Havana and me, or even just to get more than four hours of sleep a night. Instead, he was stuck on this treadmill that just kept getting faster and faster. Clay would crawl into bed late, many times after I was already asleep. I would awaken and all I could tell him was that I loved him, I missed him and I was proud of him for working so hard and for doing the right thing concerning the partnership, as we were left high and dry servicing the debt.

This time of hardship put the wheels in motion for change in our lives. Clay knew we couldn't live this way, and even if we could, what kind of life would that be? We started taking steps that would lead us in the direction we wanted to go, but we knew it would be a process to get there.

Clay's outlook improved when the partnership was successfully dissolved. His workload was noticeably lightened when he found someone to take over the business that had resulted from the partnership. With the partnership now behind him, he could go back to concentrating on solely running the entertainment company. Only now, for the first time, he had a different mind-set about the business. His goal now was to create systems that would allow the company to run and grow without him working in it. Instead of working in the business, Clay would learn to successfully delegate so that he could work on the business. This would be a monumental change in our lives.

The one thing that continued to remain absent in our lives was involving God. Yes, I had been crying out for His help, but my husband and I were not in unity on this. It was hard when Clay had the exact opposite view of wanting or even believing God could be involved in our lives. Clay always said if he could see one miracle, he would believe. God does say, "Ask and it will be given to you . . ." (Matthew 7:7). Little did he know what he was asking for at the time.

Chapter 5

How Did I Get Here?

During this crazy life schedule, I became pregnant and my due date with our second baby was quickly approaching. Our first child's birth had been induced around my due date because of a problem with the placenta. I wanted this labor to be different. I really wanted to wait until my body began labor naturally for two reasons: One, I wanted to experience spontaneously going into labor, and two, I believed that if my body had not started going into labor on its own, God didn't want the baby to come yet. I wanted to have God make the decision about when our son would arrive, not me. I felt like I would be forcing something that wasn't supposed to happen yet, and I didn't want to do that.

My husband knew my feelings on the situation, but due to the crazy work schedule he currently had, there was no way to ensure that Clay could be present for our son's birth other than to schedule it. So all work and schedule arrangements were made and labor was induced early the morning of April 23, 2007.

Aubrey Napoleon-Hill Clark was born at 3:30 p.m. weighing 7 lbs 2 oz. and measuring 19 ¼ inches long. He was perfect. Aubrey and I both checked out well and two days later we returned home from the hospital. Clay and I were excited to have another baby and a son at that. Now we had a daughter and a son. I was so happy that Clay was able to provide so that I could stay home full time raising our new baby boy and daughter. Making this possible, Clay went back into his rigorous work schedule, which had improved somewhat and for the first time the company and its employees moved into genuine office space. We downsized to a much smaller home, but I didn't mind. It was a home just for us for the first time since we had gotten married six years earlier. It was surreal. I had a 100 percent private home for just our family! I was ecstatic that I no longer had to share our home with random DJ's who worked with my husband.

With our first child, Havana, I had been a typical first-time mom. I was overly protective and couldn't stand to ever hear Havana cry. If she cried day or night, whatever the reason, I nursed her. As a result she hadn't learned to settle herself to sleep. She was dependent on me to nurse her to sleep. As a result, we let her sleep with us. This lasted for almost a year when I finally had to move her into her own bed because I could no longer deal with the lack of sleep due to her waking throughout the night needing her human pacifier, which was me.

Moving Havana to her own bed and adopting a new sleep routine was traumatic. Probably more so for me than for her. I felt terrible listening to her cry from her crib. At this point, she was old enough to stand and cry "MOOOOOOM!" I would check in on her and she was physically okay, but she was mad. It took a good week of this new routine until the crying subsided and Havana embraced her new bedtime reality.

Learning from this valuable experience, I vowed that the next time I would do things differently. A book had been recommended to me by my Aunt Karen called, On Becoming Babywise. I read it and knew I had to implement its strategies. I greatly valued my Aunt Karen's advice on the subject as she had raised four kids of her own, and the extended family had always been amazed at what great sleepers they all were. She could easily go out and have sitters put her children down without a struggle. They could take family trips and bedtimes were not a battle. Babies did not need to be laid with nor were they dependent on being rocked or nursed only to rouse sometime in the night and need to have the process repeated in order to fall back asleep. What really sold me on the book was the fact that my aunt claimed she had never had to go through the initial "cry yourself to sleep" process with any of her kids in order to reach these enviable results. She simply implemented the book's sleep strategies from the day her babies came home from the hospital. That way there were no unwanted habits created that she would later need to break. The baby was simply trained with the desired sleep habits from the beginning.

Upon Aubrey's arrival, I immediately put to use the strategies the book recommended. Aubrey was a great nurser and the schedule worked well. He was able to peacefully settle himself to sleep in his bassinet and soon was sleeping through the night. However, when Aubrey was awake, he seemed to be somewhat of a needy baby.

Our first child, Havana, had been a happy, easy going baby, other than the whole sleeping debacle. Early on she was content just to lie on her back and take in the sights and sounds as we would set up baby toys all around her. She would be situated on her back flailing her arms and legs as she cooed. Aubrey could not have been any more different. He was very attached to me and never wanted to be put down. If he was set down, he cried immediately. It didn't matter what was set up to entertain him, he had no interest. He just loved to be held. I believe he did well with his bed since he had been conditioned since birth to sleep in it. I imagine he easily recognized the familiar feel and smell of his sheets as well as the noise of music and the fan, and associated these cues with going to sleep.

As the weeks of Aubrey's life progressed, we noticed his eyes constantly moved. He seemed to continually assess the environment around him. He never stopped looking around. We were amazed at his interest in his surroundings, his desire to just take everything in. The movement in Aubrey's eyes was so obvious that the guys at the office lovingly referred to him as "scantron," because Aubrey's eyes unceasingly scanned the room back and forth, back and forth.

I didn't remember exactly when babies start to make eye contact, but I knew from previously having a baby that it doesn't happen right away. It takes a little bit of time. I honestly had no concern about Aubrey's health in any way.

Soon Aubrey went to his two-month, well-baby doctor's checkup. It was an uneventful visit, an expected formality consisting of brief questions, an exam and a heart-wrenching shot. Then we were back in our daily routine. Life had settled down. I loved the peaceful seclusion of our new home. We had adjusted to life with our new baby.

At this point, daily life involved me holding Aubrey for a majority of the time as I went about our activities. The notable exceptions were driving in the car when he was content riding in his car seat carrier, being carried in his carrier various places and when he was napping or sleeping peacefully in his crib. Outside these times, if Aubrey was not physically held, he would get upset and begin crying.

There is a specific instance in which I remember I had scheduled to have a mole removed. I took both kids with me to the appointment like I usually did. Aubrey was probably about two-and-a-half months old at the time. He had been peaceful in the carrier car seat in which I had brought him into the office. As we waited our turn to be called back for our appointment, Aubrey got antsy and I got him out of his carrier to hold him. Of course, he was perfectly content being held in my arms. We were soon called back and settled into a room. I continued to hold Aubrey as we awaited the doctor's arrival. When it came time for the procedure to take place, I had to place

Aubrey back in his infant car seat as I couldn't hold him while I underwent the procedure. Any other baby his age probably would have been happy to be placed in a car seat where he could sit, observe the action and be entertained by his older sister for the five minutes that was needed to remove the mole.

However, Aubrey, upon leaving my arms, immediately started screaming. Not a cry like you would expect from most babies when they are upset, but screaming. He was wailing inconsolably to the point where nurses came into the exam room just to pick him up and hold him as I lay helpless to comfort him across the room on an exam table. Despite the nurses' soft, soothing words and warm embrace, they were unable to console him. The outcry continued even though I was no more than four feet away from him. I kept saying, "I'm right here. Mommy is right here, Aubrey." I looked on as the nurses tried to talk to him and bounce him in their arms, all to no avail.

The five minutes I was unable to hold Aubrey felt like an eternity as we endured his cries. The moment I was released, I rushed over and the nurse holding him politely, and I'm sure thankfully, passed him to me. He quickly settled himself, comforted to be in my arms. I felt terrible. I was so embarrassed that my son had screamed the whole time and neither I nor anyone had been able to console him. I felt terrible for my son that he was so upset. Not knowing anything at this point about Aubrey being completely unable to see, I just figured he was highly attached to his mom. I had always been told that every child is different, and sons usually have a greater attachment to their mothers than daughters do. I now believed that this was clearly the case with my son.

About the time Aubrey was reaching three months of age, I planned to attend my brother Adam's wedding in Utah. Adam is an older brother to Justin and me, yet we never knew him until we were in high school. My parents had given him up for adoption years before they got married as my mom had him when she was only sixteen years old and knew she would be unable to provide the care that he needed. I had known about my older brother for as long as I can remember. I remember every year my mom crying on October 15th, Adam's birthday, and telling us to never have sex until we were married, because it had resulted in her having to give up her baby. She wanted us never to have to go through something like that. She had said giving up her baby was the hardest thing she had ever done, yet she knew it was the right thing to do.

Anyway, my mom and Adam came into contact about the time I was in high school, and shortly after that, we met him. Meeting Adam for the first time was weird. He looked exactly like a darker version of my brother Justin, yet he had a completely different personality. Where Justin and I had always been quiet, passive and reserved, Adam was funny and outgoing. My brother and Adam seemed to bond instantly. They were brothers and that in and of itself was exciting to them. Also, both excelled in athletics, so that was an instant connection point. Although I love my brother and I was excited to meet him, we didn't seem to have any shared activities, interests or values, so we failed to form any kind of meaningful bond.

Because of Clay's crazy work schedule, he wasn't able to attend the wedding with me as he DJ-ed weddings himself every weekend. But my brother, Dad, Mom and many of my aunts and uncles would attend. I was excited to go to the wedding, but I hated the idea of traveling without Clay and missing him that weekend. I was so grateful to have my brother Justin traveling with me and the two kids.

Upon arriving in Utah, I was anxious to see all my aunts and uncles. I had seen many of them six weeks earlier at my cousin's wedding in Dallas, so they had already met our new baby. I have always enjoyed spending time with our extended family.

My grandparents, Gram and Da, had driven in their RV to the location of the wedding. When they travel anywhere, they use the opportunity to make a cross-country vacation out of it by taking scenic back road routes in their RV and arriving at their destination using their vehicle as a traveling hotel. Although the wedding was taking place in their home state of Utah, they didn't miss the opportunity for all the family to convene together in their RV.

I remember how my aunts oohed and awed over little Aubrey. Characteristically, my mom wanted to hold him right away. Not considering how her words might offend me, she blatantly asked, "What is wrong with his eyes?"

I remember it like it was yesterday. "What do you mean, what is wrong with his eyes?" I had seen Aubrey every day since he was born. Therefore, I never noticed a change in his eyes. To me they had always moved in the fashion that they were now. There had never been a difference in his eye movement that I had noticed from one day to the next.

"Why are they moving like that?" she questioned.

"He is looking at everything. He always does that," I said. I was a bit annoyed with the questioning, implying that something was wrong.

My mom continued, "That is not right. His eyes are not supposed to be doing that. They weren't doing that at Megan's wedding. When did this start?" Now turning to others she asked, "Do you all remember Aubrey's eyes moving like this at Megan's wedding?" She proceeded to ask everyone who was gathered with Gram and Da in the RV.

I was beginning to feel a bit flustered. She didn't even know what she was talking about. But she just kept asking me questions about his eyes. "He has always moved his eyes like that. He loves to look around," I said.

She persisted, "I don't think he was doing that at Megan's wedding. You don't see that?"

"Mom," I said, "I see them moving. That is how he has always moved his eyes." This was the first time anyone had brought up any concern about the movement of Aubrey's eyes. I was annoyed that my mom wouldn't let it go. Why was she saying something was wrong with Aubrey's eyes? Surely if that was the case I would know or his doctor would have said something.

I don't remember anyone else chiming in, worried over the movement of Aubrey's eyes. Many of my aunts were together with us in the RV, and my mom was openly voicing her concern. They all saw Aubrey, so looking back I assume they all had noticed. I think they must have not wanted to upset me. Obviously, it had been said to me that there was movement in Aubrey's eyes. What more could be done?

Soon we went our separate ways in preparation for the wedding ceremony. The ceremony was to be held outdoors. The location was garden-like with large rolling hills covered in green grass and dispersed with various walking paths that were lined with flowers, plants, fountains and swings. It was beautiful. The guests' seating was arranged on one such grassy area that was the most level. A brick walkway led downhill to the seating and would be where the wedding attendants and eventually the bride herself would walk through until she reached the place in the grassy expanse where she would say her vows.

As the ceremony began, I took in the beautiful setting. I could see the ceremony from where I stood, yet I didn't sit with the other guests as I held my young son and did not want to be a distraction.

Midway through the vows I made my way the short

distance over to the reception site as Aubrey was getting antsy, and I didn't want to cause a disturbance during this special time. I also had Havana with me. We had intended for her to participate in the ceremony as a flower girl, but while getting ready I had accidentally burned her with a curling iron, and she hadn't emotionally recovered in time to make her appearance.

I remember how unique the reception hall was. In keeping with the outdoor garden theme, it reminded me of a greenhouse. There were floor to ceiling windows. Actually it would be more correct to say that all the walls and the ceiling of the structure were made of glass and simply connected to one another, adjoined by whatever small vertical piece of metal that connected each large window pane to the next. Inside the structure there was lush tropical greenery and exotic, brightly colored flowers. Various fountains added to the ambiance as the hanging lanterns and lights reflected off of the water and the sound of it flowing became a part of the peripheral noise. Looking up at the encapsulated ceiling, I saw that thick vines climbed up the entire structure, floor to ceiling, top to bottom. I was inside an indoor structure, yet there was thick, dense foliage that seemed like a mini rainforest. It was very moist inside and cool, not hot and uncomfortable. Holding Aubrey I walked around the tables and I reserved a place for myself to sit. It wasn't long before the crowd came teaming in, escaping the heat. Various family members filled in the table I was sitting at.

Shortly after we had eaten dinner, my Aunt Katherine, who is a pediatrician in California, took a moment to pull me aside. We had our privacy. By nature Katherine is a nurturer – kind, loving, giving and soft-spoken. Softly and calmly she advised, "Vanessa, you really should take Aubrey to see the pediatrician when you get back." Immediately I was alerted. This was not just someone spouting off random, unwarranted, ill-informed concerns. This was someone whose job was evaluating children's health, and she was telling me I needed to see our pediatrician.

"What do you mean? We were just there for his two-month checkup and everything was perfect." That was what Aubrey's doctor always told me: "Perfect! Your baby could not be more perfect!" He would not have said that if there were any concerns. I pressed her further to find out exactly what was going through her mind.

"Why? If there was something wrong, wouldn't the doctor have told me?" I questioned.

My aunt hadn't brought up any concern earlier that day when my mom had been grilling me in the RV. Likewise, I had dismissed all concern. No one else had been worried. It had just been my mom. But now with my aunt pulling me aside, obviously she was concerned. Why should I have to take my son to a doctor? She was a doctor. If she knew something was wrong, she needed to tell me what it was. Why should I have to wait for a scheduled appointment?

Suddenly as I pressed for information, sweet Katherine seemed to pull back and retreat. "Well, I just think it would be good for him to see his doctor. Do you go for regular checkups?"

I felt attacked. Of course I take my kids for their doctor appointments, I thought. Aubrey just had his two-month checkup four weeks ago.

"His eyes really shouldn't be moving like that. It's not natural," Katherine stated.

What do you mean, not natural? Come on, say what you mean, I thought. I have no idea what you are talking about.

"I mean, something is causing his eyes to move like that."

"What do you mean, what is causing his eyes to move? Aubrey is not making his own eyes move."

"Well, I don't know. I mean, I can't say. It could be anything." She was trying to back off again, to be dismissive, to make me go to my doctor for answers, but I knew she had to know something. Otherwise, why prompt this discussion?

"Anything? Like what? What could it be?" She knew SOMETHING. She was a doctor and she was obviously concerned. I figured she wouldn't tell me all this if she didn't know something.

"They probably need to order a MRI and a CAT scan. It could be a tumor, something pressing in and causing the movement."

It was surreal. Here I stood in the middle of beautiful, fantasy-esque scenery. People dressed up, laughing and dancing. I was in the middle of joyous, spirited commotion, standing there talking to my aunt. All of my surroundings were suddenly out of place. I was out of place. I could not be here anymore. I needed to leave right then. I don't know in what outward emotional state I managed to leave that brief conversation, but I couldn't leave soon enough. As soon as I heard what I needed to hear, I wanted to get away.

I tried my hardest not to lose it right there in the middle of the reception as I held my baby. Obviously, the reason my aunt had been reluctant to share her concerns with me was because she had not wanted to upset me. Too late! My mission now was to get away as quickly as possible so as to not lose my composure in front of anyone. I just wanted to be alone, to be gone.

Anyone who really knows me, or who has ever seen me sit through a church service, knows that I am a huge crier. As much as I hate to cry in front of people, it's kind of funny, because I always do.

I spotted my brother Justin and made a beeline for him. He could tell that something was wrong, but he didn't know what. "Will you hold Aubrey for a minute? I need to call Clay. It is an emergency. I need to use your phone." (My phone only had coverage for the Tulsa area.) Without further explanation, I handed Aubrey to Justin and left with his phone.

Quickly I headed off to a quiet area and called Clay. Music was playing in the reception hall and its sounds and vibrations were carried everywhere. I stood in a hall just outside of the main room where the festivities were being held. The area was mostly vacant. However, occasionally a person would walk by trying to locate the nearest restroom.

"Clay, Clay, can you hear me?" He was in the middle of DJ-ing a wedding reception somewhere in Texas. I had to talk uncomfortably loud to ensure that Clay could hear me.

"Clay, Aunt Katherine says we need to take Aubrey to the doctor because there is something wrong." My voice cracked as I got the last word out and the enormity of the word weighed on me. Wrong. Something was wrong.

"What? What's wrong?" He was shouting over the music in the background.

"Go somewhere quiet and call me back." I hung up. I waited. Clay would be getting a song cued up that would be long enough for him to leave the booth for a few minutes to call me back.

The phone rang.

I answered and quickly repeated our previous conversation. Fortunately, I didn't have to talk as loud for him to hear this time.

"What's wrong?" Clay repeated.

"The movement of Aubrey's eyes is not supposed to be like it is. She says it could be a tumor, but she doesn't know. I don't know. We have to go to the doctor. I want to come home." I looked down at the ground as I spoke. Around me random guests passed by. I knew they probably could hear me. I didn't dare raise my head and make eye contact with anyone as tears were streaming down my face, and the last thing I wanted to do was to have to talk to someone. I was upset and scared. Suddenly I was annoyed. I was annoyed with all these people that they were here where I was and that I was here at this wedding. Everyone was so happy and I was expected to be happy. I just wanted to be alone. I needed to be home.

Clay was immediately upset and worried. I had no answers for him. I got off the phone quickly. I knew my brother would be looking for me, and Clay couldn't talk anyway because he had to get back to his show.

On the way back to find my brother, I ran into my dad and his wife, Jan. Obviously, they could tell that I was upset and had been crying. I stopped only briefly, mentioning something about not feeling well and continued on my way.

Upon finding Justin, I settled Aubrey who had been crying the entire time Justin held him; and I went to go find a place where I could be alone. Trying to stifle the eruption of tears that slowly spilled over, and threatened to explode at any instant, I tried again not to make eye contact with anyone. I didn't want to talk. That would really cause a breakdown. Anyone who did manage to make contact with me as I was on my way out, I quickly let them know that I was not feeling well and I had a splitting headache, which I did have at this point. My daughter Havana was being entertained by family so that was one less concern.

I needed a private place to be alone. I made my way to the bridesmaid's dressing room. It was empty as everyone was enjoying the reception by this point. The room was a little surreal to me. All white with flowers and white flowing curtains. Makeup, shoes and hair accessories were strewn about on vanities. The mirrors were lined with bright light bulbs, and they must have been emitting heat or the room was poorly ventilated, because the longer I stayed in there the hotter I got. I didn't really care though. It wasn't enough to make me leave. I just quietly sat holding Aubrey, watching girls I didn't know come in and out around me, primping in the mirror, reapplying lipstick, fixing their hair, changing their shoes and laughing about various things that had occurred throughout the evening. I was glad that they left me alone. And I was glad I didn't know any of them. That way I didn't have to talk to anyone.

The plan was to wait until a family member could drive me back to where I was staying as they were leaving the festivities. My grandparents drove me back. They had no intention to stay until midnight! My brother Justin joined me, and Havana and Aubrey were in tow.

I was thankful for my brother's familiar and supportive presence even though I hardly spoke to him during the trip back. I was exhausted, emotionally spent, and I had retreated to a world of quiet thought as I gazed out of the window at the passing surroundings. As we arrived at the home we were staying at, I thought, we are leaving tomorrow. I couldn't wait to get on the plane headed home and get everything figured out.

I don't even remember the flight home to Tulsa. I mean, I know I took a plane, but I don't recall going to the airport, traveling home with the kids or anything.

All I know is that as soon as I arrived home, I called our pediatrician.

"What is the reason for your appointment?" the receptionist inquired.

"My aunt is a pediatrician, and she saw my son at a wedding I was at this weekend. She had seen him six weeks before and wasn't concerned, but now she is concerned and says he needs to get his eyes examined, because they are moving in an unnatural way." I had successfully word vomited out all the information I could as fast as I could.

"Okay, so let's schedule an appointment." I realized the lady had no idea what I had been talking about. She simply answered the phone and set appointments.

The appointment was scheduled.

Within days we were at the doctor's office. I was glad to be there seeing someone with authority who could tell me everything was fine, just like I had heard four weeks previously and countless times before with my daughter during her well-baby checkups. Our pediatrician loved to declare, "Your baby is perfect!" upon completion of those exams. I think the pediatrician must have enjoyed saying those words and seeing mothers smile with joy and pride at their "perfect" child. I suppose all of us mothers unadmittedly and unknowingly loved hearing those words more than we realized. Now I knew how valuable that declaration was. It was what I needed to hear and expected to hear, like I always had.

Havana and I sat in the waiting room with Aubrey. My mood had settled. No longer was I the basket case that could lose it at any moment like I had been only two days before at the reception. It calmed me to know that I was at the doctor's office, the place where all the questions would be answered and all the facts would be sorted out. The doctor would fix whatever was making Aubrey's eyes move, or he would inform me, like so many other mothers' concerns, that this was nothing to worry about and my son was "perfect."

"Aubrey Clark." It was our turn. Three-year-old Havana, Aubrey and I were escorted to a room where we sat quietly while the nurse reviewed the notes on Aubrey's file.

"It says here that there is movement in his eyes?" the nurse questioned.

"Yes, my aunt, who is a pediatrician in California, just saw Aubrey this weekend at a wedding, and she said his eye movements are not natural, his eyes shouldn't be moving like they are and we should see our pediatrician."

"Okay, you were just here for his well-baby checkup. Didn't the doctor look in his eyes? Everything was okay. Right?" the nurse asked casually as she continued to view Aubrey's file.

"Yes, but she just said his eyes needed to be examined."

"Okay, the doctor will be in in a moment." The nurse quickly left and shut the door.

Again, waiting. It always takes a while for the doctor. I felt very calm and at ease. I had never been to a children's doctor and received any unpleasant news. The possibility wasn't even in my mind. It was like you just came here, the doctor would shine a light in his eyes, throat and ears; measure his height, weight and head and tell me he looked great!

"Do you have any questions or concerns?" the doctor would ask as he completed the exam.

"I didn't know about this rash that just popped up."

"Oh, don't worry about that. It will go away in a couple days. Kids get that all the time."

The visits really just seemed like a formality to me. I mean, it wasn't like this is where really sick people went. That was the hospital.

At last the doctor came in.

I told the story again. He listened patiently, then got out whatever instrument it is he uses to shine light into the pupils of Aubrey's eyes. "Normal," he says.

I knew it! I thought to myself.

But he still seemed stumped as to why Aubrey's eyes were moving. He is looking at him quizzically and focusing on his eyes.

"Does he ever look at you?"

"No, he just looks around at everything else," I said. It probably had to be a boy thing in my opinion. I had never had a boy before, but in my mind boys were probably more into things than other people. I mean, wasn't that a thing about men? More into tasks or something while women are more relational. Sounded about right to me.

"How about his sister? Does he look at her?"

"Well, no. I guess not." Suddenly I felt slightly embarrassed, as I now realized this meant he was supposed to have been looking and yet Aubrey had never looked at either of us before. I felt embarrassed that he had never looked and even more embarrassed that I had never been concerned about him not looking.

"I'll be right back."

The doctor left and quickly reentered with his wife who is also a doctor at the practice. I held Aubrey in my arms. He was positioned with his chest against me, looking out over my shoulder. Each of the doctors looked inquisitively at him. Both doctors still seemed stumped.

Although unspoken, they seemed to be in agreement that the movement was not normal. Otherwise, they would have dismissed the concern and let us go. Yet, they couldn't pinpoint anything wrong or any specific reason why Aubrey was moving his eyes the way he did.

Finally, the woman doctor pulled out a set of car eyes and jingled them near Aubrey. He made a little jumping movement against my body.

"The keys, I don't think he knew they were there. I don't think he knew about the keys. The noise surprised him," she exclaimed.

I was not surprised by Aubrey's reaction. Unexpected loud noises scare babies all the time. The doctor didn't seem alarmed, but contemplative.

"I am going to give you the number of a pediatric ophthalmologist, and he will be able to help you. Give us a call and tell us what he says."

I was handed a yellow sticky note with a name and number scribbled in the doctor's scrawl. I thanked the doctors and left. The doctors had seemed stumped, but not overly concerned, and so my mood mirrored theirs.

I made Aubrey's appointment with the specialist as soon as I got home. We were able to get in quickly. It was within days of the pediatrician visit. I was anxious to put all these doctor visits behind us. Clay's mom, Grandma Mary, was able to watch Havana so I was able to take Aubrey to see the specialist by myself.

I arrived at the office and checked Aubrey in. There weren't many people in the waiting room, just a couple of parents with young children and babies waiting to be seen. I didn't put much if any thought into what an ophthalmologist actually was. Personally, I had never worn glasses or contacts. Within a short period, Aubrey was called back and examined.

I remember very little details from this actual exam. It seemed extremely quick and simple. It mainly consisted of shining light into my son's eyes and having him follow various objects and cards, mainly black and white in color. After the exam, the doctor asked me to follow him. He led me to another small exam room at the end of the hall that had a phone on a table. The specialist politely said, "I need you to call your husband and have him come to the office," to which I replied, "No, it's okay. He can't. He's working."

Sternly, the ophthalmologist said, "No, I need you to call your husband right now and have him come to the office." He then left the room and closed the door. I stood there looking at the closed door and felt my eyes begin to fill with tears. I am crying even now as I remember those words. Those are the words that cut into my soul like a knife and told me that something was devastatingly wrong.

Chapter 6

The Diagnosis

Making this call to my husband was devastating. It signaled that something was terribly wrong. Something that would be too much for me to handle on my own. I never called Clay at work. I just didn't do it. When he was working, he was working. I dealt with home stuff. He dealt with work. Besides the birth of our two children and the doctor's appointments during my pregnancies, Clay had never been to a doctor's appointment with us. I had never expected him to or saw a reason for it. That's just how it was. Making this call disrupted the way we traditionally took care of our affairs, and I knew it indicated that something bad was about to happen.

I picked up the phone and called my husband. Immediately as I spoke the words, "Clay, the doctor wants you to come to his office where we are right now," I began to sob. I don't know how talking was connected with my ability to keep my composure, but as soon as I opened my mouth, the floodgates had opened as well as I was filled with a sense of dread about what was to come.

"What is wrong? What did he say?" Clay anxiously inquired.

"He didn't tell me. He just said that you had to come here now," crying more as I spoke and uncontrollably gasped for air.

Quickly, I got off the phone with my husband so he could make his way to meet us. I waited alone in the exam room silently holding my son, who snuggled contentedly against me as I held him. I paced the small room with his little three-month-old frame in my arms. He liked the movement. As I walked, I focused on keeping my composure and making sure that all traces of crying were gone before the eye doctor would see us again. Since I was no longer on the phone with my husband having to speak, I could successfully hold in any new tears. I wiped away all the old, smearing them across my face with my hands. Soon my face was dry. However, there could be no mistaking my puffy, bloodshot eyes. I felt numb. I didn't know what to think. I didn't even know the possibilities of what to think. Here I was, waiting in fear. I had already been crying and I didn't even know what the doctor would say to us, but I knew whatever it was, it had to be serious. I could feel it. I sensed it in the forceful way the doctor had commanded me to get Clay to come immediately.

The one thing that never entered my mind was Aubrey having a vision problem. Every time a doctor had looked at his eyes, his eyes had always reacted in whatever way they were supposed to. I had never been alerted for any reason to have concerns in this area. In the back of my mind I knew, but didn't want to remember what my aunt had said concerning a tumor. It was a sinking thought.

The door opened and it was Clay. I was glad to see him. Somehow having him there with me was a relief in itself. He could tell I was holding back tears. I had been waiting alone for close to a half hour at this point. Shorty after, the specialist came in. The mood was somber. Clay and I were quiet, waiting for whatever it was the doctor had to tell us. He didn't stall, but got straight to the point. "Baby is not seeing," he said factually like, "the sky is blue." It was a statement void of emotion, but for Clay and I, the statement was monumental.

It might seem like it should have been obvious to me, but it honestly never occurred to me that Aubrey might be unable to see. I couldn't believe it. It didn't seem real or even possible. How could I have a baby who couldn't see? How could I not have known?

The statement meant more than the few words contained in the sentence that my son being held in my arms was visionless. The statement meant our whole lives would change. Dreams I never even knew I had were being destroyed right in front of me – the dreams I unknowingly had and had taken for granted for my son's life. To grow up playing with friends in the neighborhood, to compete in sports, drive a car, take a girl on a date and eventually experience a wife and children of his own. All of this would be different now. It wasn't fair. I didn't want to believe it.

Always the entrepreneur and problem solver, Clay wanted to get off the problem and onto the solution. He wanted to know the plan of action, what our next step would be. "What do we need to do?" Clay asked. "What sort of treatment or surgery do we need to sign up for?" Immediately we had assumed as the doctor revealed the diagnosis, he would naturally go on to inform us as to the treatment plan to remedy the problem. However, what followed shattered us.

"There isn't any solution," he calmly stated.

I started crying. Silently crying.

"What do you mean? There has to be something. LASIK? What about eye transplants? There has to be something," Clay enthusiastically challenged.

"No. Everything looks great in Aubrey's eyes. His ocular nerve isn't too small, his retina looks great, so there is nothing to fix. The problem has to be caused on the cellular level, a cone or a rod and there isn't anything that can be done to fix any of that." He went on explaining the cold facts that were now a reality. "He was born this way. There is nothing that can be done to repair it. When babies are born, their vision isn't great. It develops over time. When Aubrey never started seeing, by default he developed what we call nystagmus. That is what the involuntary movement of his eyes is called. It is like his eyes needed something to do."

The unnatural eye movement was the reason we were even at the specialist's office, – nystagmus, so that's what it was called. We were there simply to see about his eyes moving, and now the doctor says he can't see?.

Still trying to take this all in, to process it, I questioned, "How could he have been born this way? What caused it?" There had to be a cause, an explanation. Something like this can't just happen. "A vitamin deficiency or exposure to a toxin or something?" I was trying to think back through my pregnancy, trying to recall anything unusual that might have happened. "Maybe I had an alcoholic beverage before I realized I was pregnant. Could it be fumes from the gym floor they were redoing at the high school I had coached cheer at the year before? I thought I had stayed away from them, but anything is possible."

"No, it is a genetic thing. Are you done having kids?"

Clay and I looked at him blankly and then at each other. We hadn't really thought about it yet.

"If you have any more kids, there will be a one in four chance they will have the same problem," he stated.

"But it can't be. I mean, we don't have a history of blindness on either side," I protested. He definitely is mistaken here, I thought.

"Everyone carries genetic flaws. It doesn't mean they automatically manifest. You would have to marry someone with the same genetic flaw as you. That is extremely improbable, like a one in a million chance, and then the genetic flaw would have a chance to manifest, but it might not."

"Surely they are working on something." Clay was still holding onto hope that there was something we could do or something that the ophthalmologist could do.

"They have state programs that can help you out. They can help you find the best ways to care for him and to help him learn," the doctor said.

"So you mean he will never see?" Clay pressed on.

"He has absolutely no light perception. He sees nothing. The best you can hope for is that perhaps he may be able to see shapes and shadows at some point, but never details or faces," the specialist dryly stated in a ruthlessly honest sort of way.

We were both crying. The doctor had painted a clear picture for us, brutal but clear.

"I'd like to pray with you. News like this can destroy a family," he said sincerely.

We huddled in to be led in prayer. I felt completely numb. "Lord, I ask that Clay and Vanessa come together in this and are not torn apart." That was the gist of the prayer, basically for our relationship and family unity. I am glad that he did pray with us. It was the right gesture and I believe it was heartfelt, but it sure didn't make me feel any better.

Sharita and I pregnant with our sons.

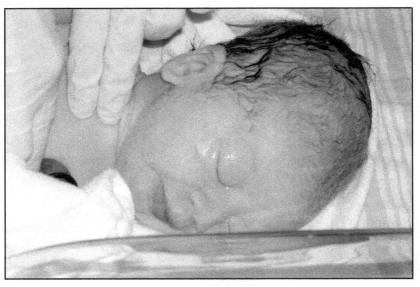

Aubrey after he was born.

Clay and Havana with newborn Aubrey.

Clay and I at a party with Aubrey at 6 weeks old.

*Aubrey (6 weeks old) with me
at my cousin Megan's wedding.*

Aubrey (pre-vision) and Clay.

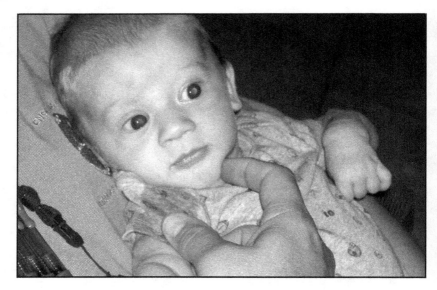

Aubrey (pre-vision) about 2 months old.

*Havana and Aubrey at Havana's 3rd Birthday party
with Grandma and Grandpa Clark.*

*Havana, Aubrey and I in Destin, FL
on the trip when he was starting to see.*

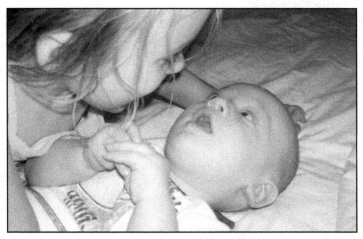

Havana interacting with Aubrey on the Destin, FL vacation.

Aubrey and Havana on the vacation to Destin, FL when Aubrey began to see.

Clay with Aubrey after he started seeing (around 4 1/2 months).

Aubrey sees!

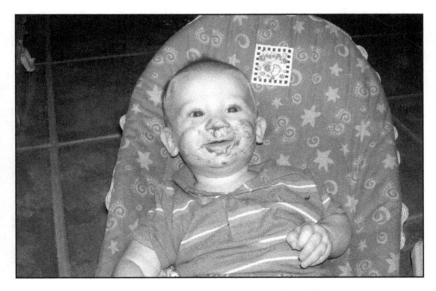

Aubrey smiles (about 5 months old).

Aubrey (about 6 months old) with his sister, Havana.

Aubrey (seven and a half months) and Havana,
pictures for Christmas 2007.

Aubrey with glasses, about 8 months old.

Aubrey about 8 months old.

Aubrey about 4 years old.

Clark kids spring 2013.

Aubrey ready to play hockey, age 6.

The Clark Family.

Chapter 7

Darkness

Our world had been rocked. Everything had changed. I held my son and felt terrible. Terrible for all the times I had put him down thinking that he was just a more "needy baby." Of course he had been needy. He wanted me when he was placed down. He had no idea where I was or where he was. According to the doctor, Aubrey didn't even have light perception. He was essentially living in complete darkness.

And into the darkness is where my husband and I both went as well. Clay oscillated between uncontrolled outbursts of tears mid-workday and outbursts against God. Clay was very angry at God. He reasoned that a God who could allow this to happen could in no way be considered good. What had Aubrey ever done? He was just a baby. He reasoned that either God was not good as He allowed something like this to happen or not powerful as He didn't stop it. Either way, Clay wanted no part of Him.

Again, like at the wedding, I wanted to retreat into aloneness, but there were questions that had to be answered. Our family knew we had this appointment and as much as I wished I didn't have to tell anyone about anything, they asked questions.

"So what did you find out? What did the doctor say?" Immediately I had to answer the question as I arrived to pick up our daughter Havana from my mother-in-law after the exam.

I did my best to be as nonchalant as possible. "They say he is just having trouble seeing." That was it. That was my reply to anyone who asked. I didn't consciously decide to answer this way. I just never would say that he was blind. I never said it and I didn't offer any further explanation at the time. I am sure word got around quickly though from anyone who inquired from my husband. He told them what the ophthalmologist had said.

I got a lot of other questions too from my mom. Maybe others felt the same way and never said anything. I am not sure, but for whatever reason my mom felt empowered to ask questions that oftentimes felt like accusations. What did I eat during my pregnancy? Did I always remember to take my prenatal vitamins? Statements that things like this happen if you don't eat the proper diet while pregnant. It was implied that I was the cause of my son's condition. It was very hurtful and I believe it was an unfair burden for anyone to be carrying at such a trying time – trying to defend myself and my innocence in our family's current circumstance when I was just trying to make it through each day. Maybe since she hadn't seen my tears as I never cried in front of anyone other than the doctor that initial day, she believed I was strong enough to handle her truth. But it was destructive. Don't you think that I, more than anyone, wanted my baby to be healthy? To somehow imply that I had been the cause of my son's problem was gut-wrenching. Thankfully, I was continually reassured by doctors that this was not even possible with the condition we were dealing with.

We had a referral to the Dean McGee Eye Institute by our specialist. He wanted Aubrey to have an exam on a machine that he did not have at his practice that would help clarify what was going on with the rods and cones in our son's eyes. We did not fully understand how this machine would help us at the time, but we went because we were told to and really we would have done almost anything they told us to out of our desire to help Aubrey.

After traveling to Oklahoma City and enduring almost a full day of waiting due to our paperwork being misplaced, we saw a very nice doctor who conducted an eye exam and then politely informed us, "Yes, everything you have been told by your specialist is true." He informed us that Aubrey could not see and there was nothing that we could do about his vision. They were not able to use the machine we had made the visit for because it was out for repair.

After talking with this specialist, I didn't really understand why we wanted to have this test done anyway. It didn't make sense, because I asked how the information from the results of the test would help Aubrey's vision (still believing there had to be something we could do), and they informed us that the results would simply clarify the cause of his condition, specifically a cone or a rod problem. After finding this out, we decided it was unnecessary for Aubrey to endure this painful test in the future.

Clay began taking action in the ways he knew how. He tried to find out what could be done for Aubrey. In this process he was informed of a local school that helped blind children. He told me that there was a waiting list and I needed to put Aubrey on it right away. I never did. I didn't even consider it.

Maybe you could say I was in a state of denial, I don't know. However, I knew the circumstances we were living in. I knew the day-to-day challenges we faced, because I lived them. I just knew that this would not be my life. I knew this was not what God or I had for my family.

I saw Havana trying to interact and play with her brother, only instead of the joy of watching your children play together (which is one of the greatest joys I believe any mother can have), Havana's attempts to interact with her only sibling were met with nothing. No reaction. It hurt that she didn't even know how her interaction with her brother should be.

The doctor's diagnosis changed everything, but it empowered us in many ways. I knew now why my son always cried when I had to put him down. Now that I knew, I tried to always hold him. I was afraid that if I put him down he would feel alone and abandoned. Immediately I brought him into our bed so he would no longer have to sleep alone at night. Clay brought me CD's filled with orchestral movie scores that we would play constantly, whether in the car or at the house, to comfort and stimulate Aubrey. We gave Aubrey lots of baths. He loved them. We theorized this was because he felt safe as the water enveloped him. Along this theory someone I met mentioned to me that she had known a baby who had a vision problem and he had loved having a three-sided box placed over him as the inside was covered with all sorts of different textures and things for him to feel as a way to explore. I guess it would be a version of a baby gym for the visually impaired. I intended to make one for Aubrey.

My days were filled, as they always had been since the birth of our first child, caring for my children. I was kept busy and would appear for the most part to be holding up well. I was constantly busy. I would wait for those moments when all was quiet. When Aubrey was napping and Havana played quietly in her room, I would go to my bedroom, shut the door and just cry and cry and cry. I would tell God everything. I never doubted that He heard me. I never doubted that He could help me, but I wanted Him to do it. So I cried and I begged and I pressed in.

I didn't have to think back to all the healings I had witnessed while at O.R.U. The foundation had already been laid. They were in me. The belief was there. I knew it COULD happen. Now I just wanted it to happen.

I didn't know what else to do, so I sought God relentlessly.

Chapter 8

Search for Truth

Upon returning from that fateful doctor's visit, not only were we bombarded with the questions of others, but I had questions of my own. I needed answers and immediately I turned to God.

As I returned home, running through my mind over and over was, "Why was this man born blind? Why was this man born blind? Why was this man born blind?" I knew that phrase was somewhere in the Bible. As Aubrey lie asleep after our eventful morning and Havana played quietly in her room, I feverishly scoured through the New Testament, flipping back and forth through the pages. I had never been a big Bible reader, just a little here and there. I didn't even know all of the books of the Bible and certainly not their order, but I knew it had to be there. It had to be in the New Testament since Jesus healed the man, but what did He say? What was His answer? Why was the man born blind? Why? It was suddenly vitally important to know the answer. I knew it was there somewhere . . . and then I found it.

"His disciples asked him, 'Rabbi, who sinned, this man or his parents, that he was born blind?'

'Neither this man nor his parents sinned,' said Jesus, 'but this happened so that the work of God might be displayed in him'" (John 9:2-3).

I cried and cried as I read that verse again and again, over and over. I lie sobbing on my bed, the Bible open before me, the page wet with my tears. The verse was so personal. I knew what it meant. That one verse told me so much. A weight lifted off of me. It was like God was telling me, "It is not your fault," and even more astoundingly it confirmed that the purpose for my son being allowed to be born this way was for God's work to be displayed. God was in control. He had a plan, a purpose. A charge of energy pumped through my body. Hope. I knew if God healed Aubrey that would certainly display His work. The Word of God had ignited hope and sparked faith in me. I was excited. Giving the verse even more significance in my mind was the fact that Jesus Himself was the One who gave the answer to the disciples. There could be no misunderstanding here.

Over the course of days and weeks, I pressed into God in prayer. In tears, in cries, in grief I sought Him. There was nowhere else to go. Doctors and the medical community had unanimously said they had nothing to offer us. Friends and family, though well intentioned, could offer comfort, but they could do nothing to fix my son's vision. For the first time, my husband, who had always been my rock, who could conquer the world, fix any problem, outwork anyone and come up with a solution to anything, could do nothing. Not only was there nothing that Clay could do, but he had decided that there was nothing God could or would do either. It would be up to us alone to help Aubrey. I couldn't believe that though. How could God allow this to happen and then leave us alone? He wouldn't do that. He had to be here somewhere. But where was He? Where was His visible presence? His audible voice? I know He says He is always with us, He never leaves us, but I felt alone, abandoned.

If God was present, I certainly couldn't feel Him. Why wouldn't He speak to me? I knew He had spoken to others. I read about it in the Bible and had heard countless accounts of God speaking to people at O.R.U. If there was ever a time in my life I thought I deserved a face-to-face encounter with the God of the universe, this was it. I would wait Him out. Other than the care of my children, I had every spare moment available to wait on God and that is what I intended to do. I didn't care about anything else. And until I got my answer, my supernatural encounter, Aubrey's healing, I would continue to see what He had to say in the Bible.

In the Bible, I read the numerous healings Jesus performed while on earth. Reading them comforted me and encouraged me. I reread the stories over and over. The Bible came to life as the magnitude of each individual's supernatural healing became real to me. These were actual people who were healed, people with hopes, dreams, doubts and emotions. People who in an instant were touched by God and their lives were forever changed.

Somewhere in my searching it came to me. Whether in thought or verse I do not remember, but it hit me deep and I knew it instantly to be truth. "With God all things are possible" (Matthew 19:26). I began to truly ponder the full capacity of that biblical statement, the implication of the meaning. ALL things are possible. The statement was limitless. ANYTHING was possible.

Another Bible verse, "God is not a man, that He should lie . . ." (Numbers 23:19 nkjv). His Word is truth. I let these thoughts, these verses from God's own Word, settle into my spirit. As I digested them, a resoluteness began to build from within. My reasoning told me that if God could not lie, then truly ALL things were possible for Him. This meant Aubrey's healing was possible! What kind of sense would it make to believe that all things EXCEPT Aubrey's healing were possible? That wasn't logical. And how could I read the Bible and take it for anything but absolute, undeniable truth if God does not lie? God's Word was confirmation of the hope and faith that were building inside of me. The words struck me deep down as irrevocable truth. As fact. Surely because with God all things are possible, Aubrey would be healed!

I became curious about others who had experienced miraculous healings. Surely there had been thousands of others who had gone before me on this journey. I began to cherish moments to myself, especially evenings when I would sit down at the computer and stay up late into the night googling "healings," "God healed me" and "God's promises" – anything I could get my hands on. I sifted through the Google search results reading countless accounts of personal stories of supernatural healing. I read verses and verses and verses of promises given by God through His Word in the Bible that had been compiled and categorized by others on the Internet.

"So then faith comes by hearing, and hearing by the word of God" (Romans 10:17 nkjv). My faith was being built. The verses spoke to me, and I made them my own. "God is not a man, that He should lie . . ." (Numbers 23:19 nkjv). I remembered that every one of these promises given by God had no choice but to be absolute truth! I cherished the scriptures that already had spoken so much to me, and I added new ones to my collection. "God is no respecter of persons . . ." (Acts 10:34 kjv). What He did for one, He would do for another.

I thought back to the healings I had witnessed while at O.R.U. and the many testimonies of healings I had heard over the years. "Jesus Christ is the same yesterday and today and forever" (Hebrews 13:8). If He healed in biblical times and has healed others, then He would heal today and He could heal Aubrey. Every verse was so deep. The implications were huge. There was much to ponder. These verses could not be read lightly, not if I actually believed what they said. What they said was life changing. The stories I read of the miraculous healings of others and their experiences with God were life changing. Reading of God's intervention in people's seemingly hopeless circumstances caused me to become more and more excited about what God would do for Aubrey. I could feel my expectancy building.

Even so, the days had turned into weeks, and my prayer for Aubrey's vision remained unanswered. Why hadn't it happened yet? This question taunted me daily. My prayers continued. As my son lie silently asleep in his crib, I would tiptoe into his room and lay my hands on him as he slept. I would conjure up the best and most heartfelt prayer I was capable of and at many times even felt I was arguing a case before the Lord. "Dear Jesus, please heal Aubrey. I know that You are the Alpha and the Omega, the beginning and the end. I know that Your Word says that with You all things are possible. I know that You are not a man that You should lie. You are the same God who healed Oral Roberts, and You are no respecter of persons, so because You healed him, You will also heal Aubrey. Thank You for being here with me and healing him. Amen."

Once completed there was nothing to do except stare down at my peacefully sleeping son. Was he healed? Had my prayer been answered? How would I even know yet, as Aubrey was asleep? I would have to wait until morning. I reasoned that an angel should come down before me so I could visually witness Aubrey being healed in its presence. Then I would no longer be in a state of constant questioning of whether or not my son's healing was yet underway. This same scene played out evening after evening in my son's room as he slept. When I wasn't directly laying hands on him, I would pray in the privacy of my bedroom alone.

During this time in my life, I really had very few friends with whom I confided. Yes, Clay and I had many great people reach out to us, who let us know they cared and were praying, but there were not many people I poured my heart out to. However, God provided the encouragement I needed through an old friend who I had cheered with at Oral Roberts University. My friend, Sharita, had a personality very similar to that of my husband, but unlike Clay, she had a strong belief in God and in His power in our lives. Sharita's ability to be candid, direct and passionate with her opinions gave her the affectionate nickname "the Shark" with my husband and me. Our friendship had grown upon completion of our cheering days at O.R.U. Sharita and I went on to coach local cheerleading squads together, and recently we had been pregnant at the same time, her with her first child, a boy, and me with Aubrey. Our sons were only six weeks apart. She had seen our family through this entire process, the pregnancy, birth and now the recent diagnosis.

Upon the revelation of Aubrey's circumstance, Sharita never seemed to be in an emotional upheaval about the situation, yet I knew she cared. She was someone I could call when I was at the end of my rope, and instead of crying with me or giving me pity, she would calmly uplift me from the dark place I was in. It was just what I needed during my "end of the world" moments. She let me know it was going to be okay. She stabilized me.

During one such phone conversation, I related the ebb and flow of my feelings and emotions that were tugging at me throughout the daily care of my children. I told her that I had this sense, this strong understanding that my son would see. The exact words I told her were, "I know this might sound crazy, but I really feel like Aubrey is going to see." I will never forget her reply. A simple statement, "If you think he is going to see, then he will see." That was it, matter of fact. She made it sound so simple. I accepted her answer as divine truth. It was the perfect encouragement I needed. I was emboldened in my belief that God would heal Aubrey.

Just as Sharita's encouragement had a profoundly positive effect on me, our son's diagnosis had a profoundly negative effect on my husband. The diagnosis had devastated him and only seemed to solidify the lack of trust he had in God. He became angry, not with me, but with God. As a husband and wife, mother and father, we remained in unity, but on the aspect of God in our lives, we were at odds. We simply didn't talk about it as it always resulted in an argument and an outburst on my husband's part. There was an inability for either of us to back down from our points and/or beliefs, because we sincerely believed them, so we just didn't venture into the arena of "God talk."

Clay knew I thought Aubrey was going to see. He simply didn't say anything to me about it. He knew it was a dangerous discussion. It was not an area he dared debate me on. It was simply too emotional. Even though Clay never said anything to me about the healing, I knew he didn't believe it would happen. I knew it by his refusal to pray or even to ask for God to intervene. I knew it by his silence when I talked about it. I knew.

At a certain point, you would think I might wonder a little bit about my own sanity when everyone around me was convinced of one reality and yet I insisted on a different one. Ironically, I never became concerned about my line of thinking. Upon reflection, this in itself might have been a cause for concern. Still I had no thoughts of myself being truly delusional, only that perhaps other people couldn't understand what I knew. Though I had no worries about my ability to function, my husband was beginning to have his doubts about me.

Thus far he had faithfully and supportively remained silent during my enthusiastic stories of others' supernatural healings and my outbursts and proclamations that surely Aubrey would start seeing. I knew he didn't truly support my belief that Aubrey would see, but he had remained silent out of respect for me. Now, as possibly a statement of hope or even a smidge of belief, Clay had something to say to me one evening regarding Aubrey's healing. "I ran into an old church friend of my parents tonight at my show (DJ-ing a wedding). His name is Steve Alley. He had heard about Aubrey and said that God would heal him."

Immediately I buzzed in excitement. Questions entered my mind and as quickly left my mouth. "What exactly did he say? How did he know? Who is he? How does he know about Aubrey?" To my knowledge I had never met Steve Alley. Clay told me that he was someone who had been a part of his family's church body during his childhood. He knew Clay's parents. Clay recalled that on several occasions growing up, he remembered that Steve had claimed to have received a word from the Lord. The spiritual stuff had always been way outside Clay's comfort zone, and as a result, he had qualified Steve as a little "out there."

"He attended church with my parents years ago, but he knew about Aubrey. He made a point to talk to me. I knew you would want to hear."

"But what exactly did he say? How does he know?" My heart started beating faster as I quizzed my husband.

"I don't know," nor was Clay interested in knowing. "Why don't you talk to him? Call my parents and get his number."

"I will, I will. I can't believe it. Well, actually I can! I am so excited! That is crazy. So you were just standing there DJ-ing. Then what? He passes by you? Or was he walking around looking for you?" Maybe he knew he had to find Clay and give him this specific message! "How did it happen?" I was talking a mile a minute as I was searching for my phone to call Clay's parents. As soon as I found the phone, I called. It took his parents a little bit to round up the number of their old friend. They had to place a couple of phone calls, but soon they called us back with Steve's number.

I called him right then and there. I was giddy and bubbling with nervous excitement. Butterflies fluttered in my stomach in anticipation of what he would say. He said Aubrey would be healed! "Hi, Steve. This is Vanessa Clark, Clay's wife. Clay's parents gave me your number.

I wanted to call because Clay said you talked to him tonight at the wedding, and you said that Aubrey would be healed! I just wanted to hear how you knew that." He seemed a little surprised that I had called, but pleased nonetheless.

"Well, no, I didn't say that he would be healed, I said he COULD be healed." Steve spoke with conviction and confidence in a slow drawn-out manner that was steady in his delivery. He was neither up nor down. He was factual in his conveyance. He had meant to be an encouragement to my husband. "I had heard about your son, and I told Clay that this is exactly the circumstance that God works in, when everyone says nothing can be done. I wanted him to know that Aubrey could be healed."

I was not impressed with the explanation. I already knew all of this. I was disappointed and didn't see the point of him telling me what God could do. I quickly thanked Steve for taking my phone call and got off the phone. Initially, I had been bursting with excitement as I made the call. Now I was let down.

This was not the answer I was expecting or looking for. I already knew everything he said. I knew Aubrey could be healed. Why would he tell us that? When I got off the phone I must have been visibly upset. Upset enough to cause my husband to break his respectful silence and now start voicing his concern. He had seen how quickly and dramatically my emotions had soared in anticipation and expectancy as we were waiting for family to get back to us with Steve's number, and he witnessed how drastically and dramatically I had come crashing down in disappointment. He didn't want to see me go through another emotional roller coaster that resulted in me being let down. He just wanted me to accept what he saw as reality and deal with it.

I was despondent, upset and near tears. I just wanted my son to see, to be healed. "I don't understand. I thought you said he said that Aubrey would be healed." To Clay it honestly didn't matter what Steve had said or didn't say, or whether or not he had a "prophetic word" from God. None of it really mattered to Clay. He had made the choice to remove himself from all hope other than that which he had in people, medicine, science and technology. But I hadn't. I was still tethered to this invisible hope, this belief that pulled me. It could bring me up in great expectation, but as long as the hope was left unrealized, it could also crush me when my expectations remained unmet. What did matter to Clay was the fact that I was upset. He saw me visibly hurt and there was nothing he could do.

"Bird, I don't think you should pray for healing anymore." He was completely serious. "I don't want to see you get upset and hurt like this."

This made absolutely no sense to me. I could not grasp what he was talking about. He didn't want me to pray, so I wouldn't be upset? But that was why I was praying, because I needed help! I needed someone to help my son, and no one could but God. What was I supposed to do?

"I just don't think it's healthy," he continued.

I could not follow his line of thinking. "Healthy? What are you talking about?" I quipped. In my mind to this day I hold the opinion that it would have been a lot less healthy for me not to pray. To simply accept defeat would bring a depressing feeling of hopelessness. Without Jesus, that is exactly where I was, hopeless. I needed this prayer, this hope.

"I mean I just don't want to see you disappointed." In Clay's mind I was living in a fantasy world. There was no hope of vision or healing. It was all made up, pretend, like magic and fairies. There was simply the reality of a blind baby boy and his mother insistently talking about the day he would start to see, while Clay looked on day by day at the unchanging situation. At this point he rationalized that it needed to stop. I had to embrace reality.

I believe to this day that even if I had it all wrong, and God didn't heal people, like Clay believed, I would rather live every day of my life in hope and in prayer, asking and truly expecting a healing, an intervention from God in a situation, versus embracing "reality" and kissing hope good-bye. Even if I never received that which I had sought, at least I could relish in the joy that it was possible that it could happen. Yes, I had lows when I didn't receive that which I waited for, but I had the highs of hope as well. I couldn't let that go.

Chapter 9

Wow! God Spoke to You?

So I was back where I started, still on the journey. The cycle of tears, prayer, hope, prayer, despair and more prayer filled my days. I had no choice but to continue to take it all to God. I knew He was the only One who could help me. I persisted calling out to Him by night and going through the motions of each day. My emotions continued their flow ranging from peaks of hope and expectancy to deep valleys of loneliness, frustration and sadness as I mourned what should have been.

On a day not unordinary from any others, I hit what my husband would have defined as a spiritual/emotional high, off the deep end! I had somehow managed to work myself up into an emotional frenzy, brought on no doubt by my daily concoction of scripture reading that had now been mixed with a testimony of supernatural healing that I had found online. I had been inspired by a specific individual's miraculous account that had been very detailed concerning the healing experience the person underwent, and I began to wonder what my own son's healing experience would entail. My imagination was running wild, anticipating, wondering and picturing what it would be like for my son when he started seeing. I mean, he had never seen anything before and imagine, suddenly he can see! What would that be like? What would he do? What would he think? Could you even fathom such an experience?

"Clay, it would be unbelievable! Just think, you have never seen your whole life . . . then BAM! Wow! How would that even be?" I paced as I inquired, passion filling my voice. "And he is a baby. I mean, he'll be blown away! Do you think it will happen all at once? He just opens his eyes one day, and there is this whole world he has never seen before?"

The excitement in the personal healing account I had just read had been transferred to me. "I'm telling you, it is just amazing to hear about these people who were healed. Their stories are unbelievable! Do you want me to read you one?"

As my husband dutifully listened to my ramblings, suddenly he nonchalantly volunteered, "Oh, I forgot to tell you. Nate said he would be healed."

Immediately Clay had my whole attention. Nate was a young recent O.R.U. graduate who worked full time with Clay on sales for the DJ business. Clay and I both liked Nate. He was clean-cut and was one of Clay's best and most ambitious workers. He was a sincere Christian who had very recently gotten married and returned from his honeymoon.

I wanted to know more. I could read more healings later. "What? He just told you that today? Why would he say that? How does he know?" I desperately asked.

It might seem bizarre to you that when people such as Steve Alley and now Nate made these statements I gave such weight as to the reason why they said what they did. In my mind, the reason why they said the statement was possibly more monumental than the words they had said. Why couldn't I just accept that they had given an uplifting word that was in line with what I believed for my son and leave it at that? If you have ever had a child who can only be helped through supernatural means, you know that such statements cannot be made without immense meaning attached to them. Unless you are someone who completely lacks any sort of empathy, you would never think of approaching a parent of a child in need and making such a preposterous statement as, "Your child will be healed," unless you have good reason to truly believe it. Without the belief behind such a statement, it would be heartless and cruel to utter such a thing, knowing it was a lie. I knew Nate and logically I knew there had to be a reason behind his declaration.

"He e-mailed me a couple of days ago. I just remembered it now."

"Why didn't you tell me? Why would he say that?" I pressed.

"I don't know."

The e-mail just said, "He will be healed"? That's

weird, I thought. Guys really don't care about details.

"Why don't you call him?" In all actuality, Clay had been angered by the e-mail and had deleted it prior to giving it any thought.

I knew Nate was a believer, and I was encouraged by that thought. I had heard that only a short while ago Nate had gone on a mission trip reaching others with the news of Jesus, and he had been amazed to witness several miraculous healings on his voyage. I quickly called him.

"Hello."

"Nate, it's Vanessa." I spent no time on small talk. "Clay said you told him Aubrey would be healed."

Casually, but confidently, he answered, "Yeah."

"Well, why would you say that? How do you know?"

"God told me," he stated.

"God told you?" I was taken aback. My eyes grew wide with excitement. "I've been praying this whole time, and God hasn't told me anything. What do you mean, He told you?"

Nate, unfazed, remained casual and laid back. "I mean, He didn't talk to me in an audible voice. It's like this. I was on my honeymoon, so like every day I would sleep in till around 11 o'clock. Thursday morning I woke up at 7:00 in the morning, sat straight up in bed and was speaking in tongues. When I was done, I felt all over that Aubrey was going to be healed, and I needed to tell Clay.

So I tried to go back to sleep. I figured I'd tell him when I got back to work on Monday. I couldn't go to sleep though, so finally I got up and had someone drive me across the resort we were staying at, which was expensive by the way, to send Clay the e-mail saying Aubrey will be healed. Then I went back to our room and went straight back to sleep."

I was on fire! Energy exploded out of my voice now, "Wow!" Then, almost pleading, "So you really think he is going to be healed!?" I begged for affirmation.

Nate's matter of fact, slightly stern response, "No. You're not listening to me."

He had my attention now.

T he line was quiet.

"I know he will be healed," he finished. There was no questioning in his voice.

And that was that. In my mind it was now settled. Aubrey would be healed! God had said so! He had told Nate!

I was on cloud nine! Suddenly I was running, jumping around and yelling out. I had an end-zone dance like I had just got a touchdown in the Super Bowl. I have no idea what could have been going through my husband's head as he watched my physical display of exhilaration. I was filled with indescribable joy. It was like Christmas morning and finding out you were getting the gift of all gifts that you had waited for so long and weren't quite sure if Santa would come through with, but then you got it! Technically, we hadn't even witnessed the healing yet, but now I KNEW we would. I was absolutely blown away. Thrilled. There it was: My son WOULD be healed.

Chapter 10

Manifestation

I spoke with Nate the week after he had returned from his honeymoon, the first week of September. The following Sunday we celebrated Havana's third birthday. Aubrey was now four-and-a-half months old. It had been about six weeks since the doctor's diagnosis. This was the day we noticed Aubrey starting to see.

Havana's party was held at our home. Joining us were a few close family friends, along with their young children, my mom and Clay's parents. During the party, my mom happened to be wearing a black and white shirt sparsely decorated with sliver bits of sequins. She sat on our couch in the middle of the festivities holding Aubrey for me, who was content on her lap as I ran to and fro hosting the party. She kept insisting that Aubrey was looking at her shirt as she held him. She would enthusiastically exclaim, "I think he is studying my shirt. Do you see that? I think he is looking at it!" As I was busy going here and there, I would glance over at my mom and smile, but I didn't give too much scrutiny as to what she was saying. I didn't have time to really investigate as I had the party to put on.

As soon as the party wrapped up and the last guest had left, I had a lot to do. Early the next morning we were leaving for a much anticipated vacation to Destin, Florida. Clay, Havana, Aubrey and I would be driving all through that next day and evening until we arrived in Florida where we would stay in a condo on the beach. It would be our first trip as a family to the ocean, and it was a much needed vacation. We were excited.

Now that the party was wrapped up, I immediately went to our bedroom to begin packing for the trip, while my mom and Clay picked up the remainder of the home from the aftermath of our celebration. Aubrey, always with me, was on his back on the bed next to my suitcase as I packed my clothes. He silently opened and closed his little mouth as he pumped his legs in the air. I grabbed a shirt covered in thick black and white stripes from my closet to place in my bag. As I did, a brief thought crossed my mind, Show it to Aubrey. Maybe it was the culmination of an afternoon of my mom insisting that Aubrey had been looking at her contrasting shirt or all of my recent research on babies seeing high contrast images before lightly colored ones. I felt like I had become an expert on the development of babies' vision.

I had witnessed on our visit to the specialists at the Dean McGee Eye Institute how they had attempted to see if Aubrey could see using black and white contrasting objects and images. He had not been able to see them, but since that time, on numerous occasions I had attempted the things I had seen them try with him in order to test his vision, especially after recent prayer sessions. I had purchased baby toys that were black and white, brightly colored and lit up. I would try to get Aubrey to follow the objects like the doctors had attempted. I had even gone on to specifically search out and purchase a mobile to place above his crib that was decorated in black and white fashion. Thus far, it had all been in vain.

Now, with the shirt in my hand, it seemed the natural thing to do was to hold it in front of Aubrey. I condensed the shirt like a rope and pulled it taunt horizontally between my two hands. Then I held it above Aubrey as he lay at attention on his back. Oddly, it seemed as if Aubrey was looking at it. My heart raced a little as my excitement peaked. I lowered the shirt down closer to him about one foot above his eyes. It really seemed like he was seeing it, but the nystagmus movement in Aubrey's eyes had been so profound that it was tricky to tell whether or not he was seeing. His eyes constantly moved involuntarily back and forth, right to left, regardless of whatever objects were before him. He was unable to follow an object like you would expect a normal eye to do in a steady fluent motion.

Still, I really thought the shirt had his attention, but the way his eyes kept moving in their regular side-to-side pattern, I could not be sure. Obviously, I couldn't ask him and I couldn't tell from following his moving eyes. As I had been holding the shirt rolled up and pulled taunt between my two hands horizontally above him, I now slowly moved it to the left side until the rolled up shirt was now being held vertically, up and down beside his head. Miraculously, Aubrey turned his head to follow it. I was flabbergasted. "Wow! Did that really just happen?" Of course, I had to do it again. Now I brought the shirt slowly back above him horizontally and then down vertically on the opposite side. He turned his head the other direction, following the shirt again as his eyes continued their regular back and forth movement all the while. He was seeing! There could be no mistake. He was actually turning his head from side to side in a direct attempt to follow the object. I didn't want this moment to stop. I had to keep showing him the shirt and moving it. It was like a dream that is so good, you wish it were true and you wish you never had to awaken from it. Only it was true. It was really happening. I wanted someone else to see what I was seeing.

I called for my mom and Clay, who were in the living room, which was only a short distance away; and they quickly came to see what all my excitement was about. They came and watched my brief demonstration of Aubrey turning his head from side to side on the bed, as he lay quietly on his back. My mom, in immediate agreement declared, "He is seeing it! He really is following that shirt. Look at him turn his head!"

Clay was a bit more reserved in his reaction. He silently took in the presentation, but didn't make a comment either way. I don't think he really understood what was going on and I think he wanted to be sure. He didn't want to encourage getting my hopes up and see me fall.

Too late! They were up, and I had no fear of them falling, because I KNEW he was seeing. I saw it!

Early the next morning we began what would be a near seventeen-hour trip, including pit stops, to our destination. I have always loved road trips with my husband as it provides hours to talk. We love to dream and make our life and family goals together. Well, we had a very specific agenda that would be played out during the drive on this trip.

A few days prior to leaving, after we had received Nate's word on Aubrey's healing, Clay and I had been perusing the aisles of Sam's Club together with our kids in tow. Due to his view on God, Clay has never been one to read spiritual books. As a matter of fact, they infuriated him and made him angry if he even attempted to read one. Clay likes to "keep it light," as he says. Delving into the spiritual cosmos provokes too many unanswered questions and leaves him upset.

Well, as we walked down a path we had traveled numerous times before (Clay is a veracious reader), a book caught his eye: God in My Corner by George Foreman. I hadn't even noticed it. "I need to get this book," Clay announced unexcitedly.

"Okay, we'll get it."

"I really don't want to though. It is going to be religious."

"Okay, then don't get it," I agreed.

"I know I am supposed to though," he said as he grabbed the book begrudgingly and put it in the cart. I didn't say anything.

So now we were in the car on our very long drive. Thankfully, the kids proved to be great travelers and slept well in their car seats much of the time. During that time, Clay had me read George Foreman's book aloud to him as he drove. The book could not have been more on-point for us. Very early on in the story, George, who did not have a relationship with God at the time, tells of praying for his gravely ill nephew out of desperation and as a result witnessing a miraculous healing transpire. I so badly wanted Clay to pray for Aubrey. I felt like somehow he was a key to the puzzle, like if Clay prayed Aubrey would instantly be completely healed, as if God had a point to prove to Clay.

As we rode in the car on that long trip to Destin, Clay prayed. It was a simple prayer, but he did pray and asked God to intervene and heal our son. I was ecstatic inside. During the car ride, I kept noticing a continuation of the prior night's event – Aubrey seeing. His eyes still moved constantly from side to side, but I could tell he could see objects, if they were held right in front of him and either were high contrast or lit up.

As we arrived in Destin and began our vacation, I began to notice other things as well. Aubrey was experiencing light sensitivity. Never before had Aubrey been aware of or bothered by bright light, or the sun shining directly in his eyes. He now would turn his head or squint his eyes if he passed by bright sunlight streaming through a window or when he was out on the beach with us. I saw it. It was happening! Over and over I excitedly told Clay he was seeing. Uncharacteristically stoic, Clay continued to keep his thoughts on the matter to himself.

Ironically as Aubrey's ability to see became more solidified to me with every passing day, this was the first time I remember feeling doubt start to creep in. I definitely could not deny that Aubrey was seeing. His behavior was changing. He was becoming a new baby, smiling and content when placed down, reaching for toys and squinting his eyes or moving them out of direct sunlight. At the same time, I was frustrated by the fact that the movement in Aubrey's eyes remained. I was suddenly gripped with fear that somehow I hadn't prayed just right. I had always asked for Aubrey to see. That had always been the focus of all my prayers. I now imagined that in some legalistic way because I had not specifically prayed for Aubrey to be healed of nystagmus, that he wouldn't be, as if God refused to heal Aubrey of nystagmus because it had not been included in my original prayers. It was a stupid thought, but it still scared me.

Regardless of what I knew in my head, the fear was still present in my heart. I didn't dare outwardly express it, but I felt it. I struggled to give the fear of this persisting eye movement over to God in faith. Every time I looked, it was still there reminding me of its presence. I tried to quickly amend my prayer, to add on to this request: "Dear Jesus, thank You for healing Aubrey of his unnatural eye movement," but my thankfulness for the healing of nystagmus felt fabricated. I was genuinely thankful for Aubrey's newfound vision, but when it came to the eye movement, instead of thankfulness I felt fear.

As our life-changing, miraculous vacation wrapped up, Clay was still unconvinced of the changes in our young son. I knew Aubrey was seeing, however slight it was. Still, Clay remained silent on the subject. I don't think he himself had seen anything that fully convinced him and fully erased any and all doubt about Aubrey's ability to see. However, that all changed in an instant.

Clay was nearing the end of George Foreman's book and actually contrary to his initial reaction, he was finding the book to be quite pleasant, relevant and relatable. Clay sat on the couch in our condo reading, holding the novel in his right hand and our young son on his lap with his left hand. Clay always makes notes, highlights and marks up the books he reads so he is able to better grasp ideas and quickly find reference points at a later time. Engrossed in the book, Clay found a point worthily of remembering. He reached for the bright highlighter and quickly brought it down to proceed to highlight the passage. As he did, curious Aubrey reached out and grabbed it. He grabbed the highlighter! There could be no questioning. He had seen it. Clay froze. What he had refused to believe now confronted him face-to-face. Aubrey could see! "Vanessa! Vanessa!" he shouted so exuberantly from the other room. "Aubrey grabbed my highlighter! He grabbed it! He can see!" I came running into his wild mass of emotion.

"I know! I know! It is amazing. He is seeing!" I agreed.

"I want you to schedule an appointment with Aubrey's eye doctor as soon as we get back and see what he says." Clay wanted to be sure Aubrey was seeing. He wanted to make it official.

I called the next morning after we returned home from vacation. Ignoring all medical practice protocol, when the office receptionist answered, I requested to speak directly with our doctor, the eye specialist. I excitedly waited until he got on the phone. I couldn't wait to give him the incredible news. He would be amazed since previously the doctor had stated that Aubrey would never see. He had stated, "Maybe shapes and shadows at best."

He was now on the line. "I need you to see Aubrey, because I think he has started seeing. We think he is looking at things and . . ."

I don't remember the exact words said by the ophthalmologist at this point. All I know is that he inferred that there was no reason to see my son since he had been examined a short time ago and it was determined that he could not see. He didn't believe me. He believed I was mistaken, and he skillfully excused himself from any further discussion. So no appointment was made to see my son. I was devastated. I felt hurt and my grief quickly turned to anger. I was livid. He had completely dismissed me. Who did he think he was? I was Aubrey's mom. I would be the first to know whether or not my son was seeing! I determined I would see the doctor for an appointment whether he wanted to or not!

I called the office back. This time I didn't identify who I was or mention the history of my prior phone conversation with the doctor only moments earlier. I simply spoke with the receptionist who answered and scheduled an appointment for Aubrey to see the eye doctor.

Jubilantly, I took my son to the appointment. I entered the exam office as high as a kite. We had just been here to receive the devastating news that my son would never see less than two months ago. Now Aubrey was seeing and I was excited to have someone officially recognize and document it. It was almost like I was showing him off. I couldn't wait for the doctor to see I was right. He was seeing! Aubrey was a different baby than he had been at our last appointment. At this point in his healing, Aubrey was able to see objects that were within about a foot to a foot-and-a-half from his face.

The doctor entered. He was reserved and quiet. He said nothing to me about having spoken with me on the phone. Neither did I bring up our conversation. He did a quick simple exam and concluded stoically, "Yeah, he's seeing for now."

Heat started rushing through my body up to my face. I hoped I was not beat red. I couldn't believe it. How dare he say such a thing. "He's seeing FOR NOW!" What kind of response was that? I knew he was seeing. The doctor knew he was seeing. He didn't deny it, but "he's seeing for now"? What is that supposed to mean? Upon inquiry, the doctor alluded that this vision might go away. He wouldn't count on it. Besides, it was so poor he was still legally blind.

I knew I would cry at any moment, not because Aubrey would never fully see like the doctor had stated. No, I knew my son was healed. I wanted to run and hide and cry because of the careless, heartless way my son and I had just been treated – like we didn't matter, like he didn't matter.

I knew Aubrey had been healed. I had been the one who personally asked God to do it. I had been the one crying on my hands and knees, begging and pleading. God had answered me and I knew it.

And I was right. Aubrey's vision continued to improve over the next months. I remember literally jumping up and down exuberant with excitement as three months later, a seven and a half-month-old Aubrey sat with his older sister on the couch, and I attempted to take their picture for a Christmas photo. From what I estimated to be about five feet away, Aubrey had been able to make eye contact with me. This was the greatest distance he had ever done that from, and I had the picture to prove he could do it. In three months he had gone from being able to see objects, one foot in front of his face to five feet now!

At his next eye appointment, the doctor still couldn't take away the fact that he was seeing, but he informed me, "He is still legally blind. He will see 20/200, maybe 20/150 at best once his vision finishes developing out. And he will never drive a car."

I was ready for the doctor and his comments this time. I didn't listen. I heard it, but silently I refused it. That prognosis was not for my son. He would see 20/20. Aubrey's eyes continued to improve. At around eight months of age, he received his first pair of glasses. His original pair were blue in color. The frames were made of a thick plastic and they strapped around his head in a goggle-like fashion. At first he really enjoyed them as they made a difference in his vision. However, during the next couple of years we went through various prescriptions as his eyes changed. Throughout many of these times he would lose interest in wearing his glasses, as his old prescription was no longer helping him. We would get his eyes checked and a new prescription made. Months later the cycle would begin again. Finally, our specialist informed us if he didn't want to wear his glasses, don't make him. If they helped he would want them.

By the time Aubrey was two, his vision was estimated to be around 20/200 and the doctor stated that it had "stabilized." At three years old, it had improved to 20/70 in each eye. Aubrey had almost completely stopped wearing his glasses at this point. It was at this appointment that the doctor said something positive to me concerning Aubrey's vision for the first time. "I am really happy with his vision. I had been hoping for 20/150 at best. I didn't expect this. I am really pleased."

Aubrey is doing great today. He is six years old as I write this. He is a determined, rambunctious, energetic child. He enjoys doing all the things most six-year-old boys do, like riding bikes, rollerblading, drawing and just having a generally great time. He has recently become very passionate about ice hockey, and this will be his first year playing in a recreational youth league.

His most recent eye exam was 20/60 in both eyes. He doesn't wear glasses and the movement in his eyes has greatly diminished. When I tell people he was born blind, they can't believe it. Aubrey has heard the story so many times. He says he gets embarrassed when I tell the story about him. We remind him how special it is that God gave him this story as a way to share with others God's love for each of us.

Chapter 11

Now I See!

I know God is continuing what He started in Aubrey, in me and in all of our lives. As we have continued to turn to Him, we move forward in all that He has for us. As Aubrey began to see, I began to see as well. Previously, I thought God had never spoken to me. I was unable to recognize His voice, because I thought God must communicate in the forms I had heard about and witnessed others receiving during my time at O.R.U. – dreams, visions, words of knowledge, etc. Yes, God can speak to people in those ways and He does, but I had overlooked that God speaks "in a still small voice," and therefore I had failed to recognize Him speaking to me. Hindsight is 20/20.

Looking back on all the events leading up to Aubrey's healing, God had prepared me in so many ways before Aubrey was even born. If I had not attended Chrysalis, been invited to college weekend at O.R.U., attended O.R.U. where I became open to the idea and belief in God's ability to heal, I would have never even known to ask for such a thing.

After Aubrey was born, He spoke to me and led me through the gut feeling that my son would see – a strong feeling from within that refused to believe the diagnosis. He spoke encouragement through a close friend to trust the feeling inside of myself. He gave me the Word of God that spoke to my spirit and built my faith. And finally, the word of knowledge given to a friend and passed on to me. Now I see that God had spoken to me the entire time. I had to learn to listen though. He led me, but I had to follow.

Since Aubrey has been healed and I have learned to recognize God's still small voice, I believe I have improved my ability to hear God. This has changed my life. I now come to God in prayer and listen for His answers in any way He may choose to reveal them.

I want to encourage you that when you press into God and seek Him, He will speak to you as well. As you reflect on your life, you may realize He has been speaking in His own way all along. He may be speaking now and leading you. Are you in tune? Do you recognize Him? Are you hearing Him? Go to the Bible. Seek and you will find. He fulfills His Word and we live by His Word. It is life to those who find it.

If you do not know about Jesus and have never asked Him to come into your life, ask Him to reveal Himself to you. If you do not know what you believe and sincerely seek Him, He will reveal truth to you.

Through Aubrey's healing, I have been given a passion to speak to others about the Lord and what He has done for me and what He can do for them. My faith and my expectancy of God's involvement in my life have been forever changed.

I know there will be skeptics. There always are. I can't explain all the intricacies of how God works. All I know is my son once was blind, God said He would heal him, and now he can see! God loves you, His Word is true and He can help you as well.

Afterword

In the time since my son's healing, I have been encouraged to pray for the healing of others in need of a miracle that only God can provide for them. Oftentimes people wonder what they can do to receive God's promises. God is not a formula that you enact and poof, your result is delivered. He is sovereign, He can do whatever He wants to do at anytime to accomplish His purposes, but it must be acknowledged, God does give us tools to use in this life to access His many blessings and assurances. Essential to procuring these promises is a relationship with the Lord, belief in the truth of His Word and promises and walking and adhering to His guidance.

Through the use of this process of relationship, God leads His people. I don't have all the answers to all the questions, but I would like to simply share the things I was led and prompted by God to do throughout the journey of my son's healing.

Accept Jesus as Your Lord and Savior

First off, it must be noted that the only reason I even had access to God's promise of healing in my life was because I was His child. I had confessed my sins and invited the Lord into my heart to live as my Lord and Savior. Even though I had done this as a young child and felt no different after I had accepted the Lord into my heart versus the moment before, Jesus had made me His and He was then at work in my life. I knew God loved me and He had the very best for me. I knew He was ever-present for me.

Do Not Accept Anything Less Than God's Promises for Your Life

At the time my son was diagnosed as being blind and hearing that the condition was untreatable, I never accepted or said the words "he is blind." At the time this was not a conscious choice I made. This was something God did in me. I don't recall initially making a decision not to say these words or speak them over my son. My line of thinking wasn't that deep at the time. I simply couldn't say the statement that he was blind. I didn't believe it. It was almost as if anger rose up from within me. I didn't believe that this could be the end of the story, and I wouldn't say that it was. I knew that this could not be what God had for my life. I knew He wanted the best for me and my family, and to me, Aubrey being blind did not fit in that picture. I would not accept it.

I want to encourage others that they do not have to accept what life throws at them either. We have a choice. Don't accept illness or disease. Don't say it and don't claim it as yours. Later, when encouraging myself with testimonies of others' healings, I learned about the power of our words. Scripture states, "Death and life are in the power of the tongue, and those who love it will eat its fruit" (Proverbs 18:21 nkjv). It makes sense to me now why I never said "Aubrey is blind." God had been working in me. I learned that saying it would give power to the diagnosis. I chose not to accept it.

Build Your Faith Through Scripture and Relationship

Speaking of God's Word, this is truly where the power to Aubrey's healing was contained. It was God's Word that initially and unwittingly flooded my mind with the question, "Why was this man born blind?" I believe as God's child, He had access to me and was speaking to me through my thoughts, even though I had yet to seek Him out in this situation. Prompted to read the story of the man blind from birth whom Jesus healed in the Bible, it spoke to me on so many levels. This is because, "The word of God is alive and active. Sharper than any double-edged sword, it penetrates even to dividing soul and spirit, joints and marrow; it judges the thoughts and attitudes of the heart" (Hebrews 4:12).

God was able to speak to me clearly through His Word. His truth resounded within my spirit. My spirit recognized His Word as ultimate truth, and it brought me clarity, peace and hope. It was something solid I could stand on and believe in. Since I was not super familiar with the Bible, I found it tremendously helpful googling "God's promises," "God healed me" and "Healing testimonies" where others referenced the words and promises of God that had helped them on their healing journey. Reading scripture is one thing, but I became empowered and encouraged as I looked up the context of the actual verses and stories that were referenced on these web sites. As I found them in the Bible, I was able to ingest the fullness of the story and scripture.

God spoke to me through His Word and strengthened my belief that indeed He could and would heal my son. I would meditate on everything I read, spending time alone, reading and rereading an individual story from the Bible and contemplating everything that it meant for my life and situation. Through this scripture reading and digesting, I was deepening my relationship with the Lord. I was spending time with Him in His Word. I felt I was getting to truly know Him and His loving character through the biblical stories that had been recorded long before my time.

Grow Your Relationship Through Prayer

After spending time saturating myself in what the Lord had to say to me through the Bible, I would then go to Him with my word, my concerns and request. At times I was hopeful and encouraged. At other times I was dejected and upset. I would talk to the Lord about all I was going through.

I believe it was during this trial in my life that I began the practice of engaging in a continual dialogue with the Lord. I know scripture says we are to "pray continually" (1 Thessalonians 5:17), but this was the first time I had ever put that verse into practice. Jesus truly became my best friend that I talked to as I went on walks, drove my car, awoke in the morning to start my day and went to bed at night. Just as you talk to your closest friend, that is what my prayer life became with the Lord, a continuous ongoing conversation. In it I would ceaselessly bring to Him my request for my son's vision. I brought before Him and repeated verbatim His Word, what He Himself had promised in the area of healing, which I now knew and was gaining confidence in.

In my prayers I referenced stories of others I had heard who had been healed and reminded the Lord what He had said, "That God does not show favoritism" (Acts 10:34). What He did for one, He would do for another.

I believe the entirety of this process of going to God, involving Him and believing Him is what led to Aubrey's healing. There is no magical formula that can be performed and viola, you are healed! God is not an equation. There is no magic potion or formula that resolves the situation. God is bigger than that, deeper than that. He is the Creator of you and me and this entire universe. He is the beginning and the end. He says, "I am the Alpha and the Omega, the First and the Last, the Beginning and the End" (Revelation 22:13). Start with Him and He will guide you to the end. Let Him infiltrate and consume your heart.

I've come to realize that no matter my need or situation, there is nothing remaining for God to do to solve it. He already provided everything I need at the cross. I don't need to beg Him or try to convince Him to help me, like I had once thought. I need simply to follow Him and accept nothing less than what He has promised for me as a believer.

Without God there is no healing. He is the missing piece. He is the only essential part of the equation. I had to start with God. I had to put all my eggs in His basket, to choose to believe His Word alone. Being saved, there is access to God. That was the first thing. I was never alone in my situation. Secondly, I used that access. I went to God. Thirdly, I inundated myself in His truth, what God had to say about the predicament I was in. Once I knew what the Lord said, I chose to take Him at His Word. I believed He could heal my son. Not without my own human doubts and worries, but the best I knew how. I asked God to help me with the rest. Scripture says, "Fixing our eyes on Jesus, the pioneer and perfecter of faith . . ." (Hebrews 12:2).

Because I kept going to God, He was able to hold my hand and walk me to victory in my situation. Anytime we go to the Lord and stay with Him, we cannot lose!